OSCAR PETERSON

THE MAN AND HIS JAZZ

JACK BATTEN

TUNDRA BOOKS

Published in Canada by Tundra Books,
a division of Random House of Canada Limited,
One Toronto Street, Suite 300, Toronto, Ontario M5C 2V6

Published in the United States by Tundra Books of Northern New York,
P.O. Box 1030, Plattsburgh, New York 12901

Library of Congress Control Number: 2011940582

Library and Archives Canada Cataloguing in Publication

Batten, Jack, 1932–
Oscar Peterson : the man and his jazz / by Jack Batten.

Includes index.
ISBN 978-1-77049-269-1

1. Peterson, Oscar, 1925-2007 – Juvenile literature. 2. Pianists – Canada – Biography
– Juvenile literature. 3. Jazz musicians – Canada – Biography – Juvenile literature.
I. Title.

ML3930.P463B33 2012   J786.2'165092   C2011-907065-0

We acknowledge the financial support of the Government of Canada through
the Canada Book Fund and that of the Government of Ontario through the
Ontario Media Development Corporation's Ontario Book Initiative. We further
acknowledge the support of the Canada Council for the Arts and the
Ontario Arts Council for our publishing program.

ONTARIO ARTS COUNCIL
CONSEIL DES ARTS DE L'ONTARIO

Design: Jennifer Lum

Printed and bound in Canada

1 2 3 4 5 6   17 16 15 14 13 12

For Ken

In researching and writing this book, I benefitted enormously from conversations over many years with the jazz pianists Don Thompson and Gene DiNovi, the jazz archivist Ken Crooke, the late jazz journalist Gene Lees, and the all-round cultural journalist Robert Fulford. I also owe much to many biographies of jazz musicians, most notably Peter Pettinger's Bill Evans: How My Heart Sings *and Mark Miller's many books. I owe much to the Toronto Reference Library and the City of Toronto Archives, and even more to the all-round editorial talents of Sue Tate.*

CONTENTS

Oscar made his sensational American debut at a jazz concert in New York's

CHAPTER ONE

OSCAR'S EXCELLENT DEBUT

On the night of Sunday, September 18, 1949, the temperature climbed to a sweltering eighty degrees Fahrenheit inside New York City's historic Carnegie Hall. All summer, intense heat had covered the city like a smothering blanket. But the oppressive atmosphere on this September night didn't bother Carnegie Hall's packed rows of excited jazz fans. They raised the hall's temperature even higher, cheering and hollering for the musicians onstage.

The players performed under the title Jazz at the Philharmonic. JATP, as it was popularly known, had been organized six years earlier by an aggressive music promoter from California named Norman Granz. Under Granz's guidance, the troupe made an annual three-month North American tour, selling out every concert hall Granz booked.

JATP's personnel of a dozen to fifteen musicians underwent changes from season to season, but it always included a core of Granz's favorites. Among those in the lineup on this night at Carnegie Hall were the sizzling trumpet player Dizzy Gillespie; the dynamic drummer Buddy Rich; and the agile and swinging singer Ella Fitzgerald.

All the JATP players were superb musicians, capable of projecting a wide range of moods. And each night, they offered a handful of gently explored ballads. But Granz insisted that his people emphasize their extroverted side. He liked battles between two drummers alone onstage, dueling against one another. And he loved tenor saxophone wars, one tenor challenging another in solos that climaxed in startling runs to the top of the instrument's range.

The musicians went along with Granz's preferences because it was clear to them that his strategy worked. Big crowds turned out for the competitive concerts; the musicians earned far more money than they were accustomed to; and Granz had made himself the most powerful man in jazz.

Oscar Peterson, sitting in the front row through the first half of the September 18 concert, wiped his forehead with a massive white handkerchief. Oscar was feeling the heat. Just turned twenty-four, he stood six-foot-two and weighed 250 pounds.

Oscar's size made him one of nature's perspirers. But the sweat also reflected mild anxiety.

In the second half of the concert, Granz was going to introduce Oscar as a surprise JATP guest artist. From Montreal, Quebec, the Canadian pianist would make his American debut in the country's most illustrious concert hall.

Only a few American jazz fans, in or out of the hall, were aware of Oscar and his music. Granz was one of the rare exceptions, having heard Oscar play in a Montreal club a few weeks earlier. He found Oscar's jazz vigorous and thrilling. Not a man to pass up a golden opportunity, Granz proposed on the spot that Oscar perform at the September JATP concert in New York.

Oscar could think of several reasons why this was a terrible idea. He didn't have a visa allowing him to work in the United States or a musician's union card that was recognized in New York City. Granz brushed off the objections. He told Oscar that his appearance at Carnegie Hall would be as guest artist. Guests didn't need visas or union cards. But Oscar insisted he wasn't yet good enough to face a demanding New York audience. Baloney, Granz said, Oscar was as ready as any musician he'd ever met.

As Oscar raised his doubts, he eventually reacted the way everybody did when Granz had made up his mind about something: He gave in.

When Oscar headed backstage during the September 18 intermission, he knew he would be playing with the JATP bassist Ray Brown. Oscar was a big fan of Brown's work. Oscar had even chatted with him two or three times, when Brown was passing through Montreal and stopped for a drink at the club where Oscar was appearing.

Now, backstage, Oscar and Ray talked about tunes they might play. As Oscar expected, the two were on the same musical wavelength. Oscar's nervous tingles slipped away. He was ready to play.

At the opening of the concert's second half, Granz, who acted as master of ceremonies at all JATP concerts, announced to the audience that he had a special treat for them – a new pianist from Canada. He gestured for Oscar and Ray Brown to come forward from the wings.

So it was that Oscar Peterson walked to center stage at Carnegie Hall for the performance that would change his life forever.

Oscar and Ray Brown played three tunes. One was a familiar Broadway show tune titled "Fine and Dandy." The second was an equally popular movie song, "I Only Have Eyes for You." And the third was a simple blues tune, which Oscar and Brown made up then and there and named "Carnegie Blues."

Virtually from the first note of the first song, Oscar had the listeners in the palm of his hand. They were enthralled, all of them taken by the sensational and fresh-sounding musician suddenly in their midst.

The audience of reasonably sophisticated jazz fans recognized that Oscar was different from other pianists of his generation. Among Oscar's contemporaries, the accepted style was to emphasize the right hand; with the left, these pianists played one or two chords in each bar while the right hand ran all over the upper half of the keyboard, throwing off single-note improvisations.

But that wasn't Oscar's way. He was a two-handed pianist, playing full and rich chords and producing improvisations with both hands. He showed phenomenal technique, getting around the keyboard in an exceptionally swift and confident fashion. Notes ran from under his fingers in near blurs. And Oscar radiated power. That might have been what most roused the audience. Oscar played hard, generating a strong, swinging beat that seemed to sweep everything before it.

The audience gave Oscar and Ray Brown enthusiastic ovations at the end of each of the two songs. But when the duo finished with "Carnegie Blues" as an encore, the crowd stood and cheered, reluctant for the two to leave the stage.

With the performance, Oscar signaled his arrival in jazz's big time. In *DownBeat*, the American jazz magazine with the largest circulation, its reviewer wrote of the Carnegie event, "Oscar Peterson stopped the Norman Granz Jazz at the Philharmonic concert dead cold in its tracks." That was the near unanimous opinion among critics and fans. Oscar was a brand-new jazz star.

CHAPTER TWO

FIVE KIDS AND ONE PIANO

F or a man who eventually reached the peak in achievement and recognition, Oscar Peterson had humble origins.

Daniel Peterson, Oscar's father, grew up in a poor family on the British Virgin Islands in the Caribbean. When Daniel was still in his teens, he ran away to sea, serving on merchant ships carrying cargos to ports in North America and across the Atlantic to England.

Daniel was bright, alert, and a sharp judge of his fellow sailors. These qualities won him promotion all the way to boatswain, a rank that put him in charge of his ship's lifeboats, rigging, and anchors. Daniel had an air of command that left the other seamen a little in fear of him. As long as he lived, Daniel never lost the ability to intimidate people, including his own children.

After a few years, tiring of life onboard ship, Daniel heard there were decent jobs on the railroads in Montreal. Canadian railroad companies made a practice of hiring only black men to work as porters on their passenger trains. Each porter's duty, as Daniel discovered when the Canadian Pacific Railway took him on in 1919, was to look after one of a train's sleeping cars. Generally, the porter was to keep his passengers happy during the rail trip. The work sounded straightforward, but it became clear to Daniel that the responsibilities were much more demanding than he ever imagined.

The porter's most basic chore – making the beds for the berths and roomettes – easily became complicated. "Some passengers sleep late, others rise early," a journalist named McKenzie Porter wrote in a *Maclean's* magazine article about the hard life of a railroad porter. "Occasionally men passengers sit up much of the night talking in the club car and go to bed just when others are getting up for their morning shave. The porter is kept on the hop to satisfy both kinds of passenger."

Each porter was expected to shine the passengers' shoes while they slept. He prepared baby formula for traveling mothers. He made early-morning coffee and served it to passengers. He dusted and tidied the car, emptied ashtrays, polished woodwork, and when the passengers went to the dining car for breakfast, he made their beds. Usually, depending on a passenger's habits, the porter had to make some beds two or three times a day. He was on call both day and night to fetch soft drinks. He needed to keep careful records of all transactions to hand in to his CPR bosses. And he answered the question that all passengers asked sooner or later: "Is the train on time?"

Oscar's first teacher was his father, Daniel (left). Daniel, who could be a tough taskmaster, wasn't always as sunny as he appears in this photograph.

The trip from Montreal to Vancouver and back, a run that Daniel Peterson made frequently, was the most grueling of all. It took four days and five nights to complete the journey one way. In each twenty-four-hour period, the porter was allowed to sleep only from 1:00 a.m. to 5:00 a.m., though often women with babies or men sitting up in the club car interrupted his sleep with calls for service. The rest of the porter's time, from the moment he woke up from his four-hour nap until the following day at 1:00 a.m., he concentrated nonstop on his chores. When the train reached Vancouver, porters were allowed two nights and a day to rest in CPR quarters before the trip back – another work-filled four days and five nights.

Meals on the train for Daniel and the other porters were taken on the fly, whenever there was time to squeeze in a quick bite. Many porters ate lightly on purpose. They had discovered it was easy to develop nervous indigestion from the constant motion of the train. For some unlucky porters, the combination of hurried meals and the rocking of the train led to stomach ulcers.

Through all the demands, porters were under orders to keep smiles fixed on their faces. They were also expected, as black men waiting on passengers who were almost exclusively white, to put up with racial insults. As far as porters were concerned, it was insulting just to be called George time after time. "George" was the name pinned on black porters through an insensitive custom dating back to the beginning of North American rail travel. Every porter would rather have been asked his real name and addressed by it. But all were black, all were stuck with "George," and they hated the name with a passion.

During the Second World War, Daniel had the experience of a white army officer going far beyond the "George" stage in his racial put-downs. The alarming incident took place late one night, when Daniel had closed the club car while cleaning and tidying it. The army officer burst into the car, demanding that "George" get him a drink. It was clear to Daniel that the man was already drunk.

Polite as always, Daniel told the officer to come back later, when he had finished the cleaning job. The officer pulled his gun from its holster. Leveling it at Daniel, he repeated the demand for a drink.

Keeping his nerves and his anger under control, Daniel walked to one end of the car and locked the door. Then he did the same thing at the other end. In his fifties at the time, Daniel was still quick and tough when he needed to be. Once Daniel had locked the car against anyone else walking onto the scene, he reached back his fist and smacked the officer in the face. Too drunk to react, the officer dropped to the floor like a stone.

Daniel lifted the officer under the arms and dragged him to his compartment, where he left the unconscious army man to sleep off his drunkenness. Daniel worried that the officer would complain about him to the CPR and cost him his job. But when he heard nothing of a complaint, he decided that the officer was too embarrassed to admit that "George" had got the better of him.

When Daniel started with the CPR in 1919, the pay for a porter's hard labor came to about ninety dollars a month plus about twenty-five dollars a month in tips. Daniel recognized that the railroad was exploiting him and his fellow porters by paying so little. But few black men in Canada earned more in other jobs. Besides, since the country wouldn't function without trains to move passengers and freight, porters could count on steady employment and regular paychecks. With these advantages, Daniel and his porter colleagues were the envy of other black men. Daniel stayed at his porter's job, supporting his family, until his retirement in the 1950s.

———

In Montreal, a year or two before Daniel joined the CPR, he fell in love with a sensible and sweet-natured young woman named Olivia John. Olivia spent her childhood on the Caribbean island of St. Kitts. In her teen years, she left school to accept a job as a housekeeper for the family of a wealthy man who owned a steamship line. Since the company's headquarters were in Halifax, Nova Scotia, Olivia uprooted herself from St. Kitts and moved to Canada. Her housekeeping chores took up most of every day and much of the evening. The pay amounted to a mere five dollars a month plus room and board.

After a year or two, Olivia decided she could do better somewhere else. She traveled to Montreal, where she worked as a housemaid in upper-middle-class homes. The jobs were equally demanding, but paid slightly more money.

Olivia and Daniel married in 1918 and brought five children into the world in the following ten years. Fred came first in 1919, Daisy a year later, then Chuck another year after that. Oscar was born on August 15, 1925, followed a couple of years later by May, the last of the kids.

For all of the years the family was together, they lived in rented houses in Montreal's working-class St. Henri neighborhood. With its old limestone houses, St. Henri was home to most of the city's two thousand black citizens. About ninety percent of the black men worked for the railroads. Since the two major rail lines, the CPR and the CNR, operated out of Windsor Station, a short walk from St. Henri, it made a convenient neighborhood for railroad families.

———

No matter how many hours Daniel put into the demands of his porter's duties, it was still tough to make ends meet at home. With so many mouths to feed, the Petersons were perpetually short of money. Often, when Olivia could arrange for someone to look after the kids, she took jobs as a maid for families in Montreal's posh Westmount neighborhood.

When Oscar was a teen, he loved to show his stuff at the piano to the other kids. The enthusiastic group in this photograph flocked to see him at a youth club in Toronto.

Both Peterson parents worked desperately hard, but there still came times when the family had little food in the house. Olivia told the kids to stay in bed on those days, in the hope they would sleep through the ache in their empty stomachs. A female friend of Oscar's from his early days said that her own family was poor when she was a child, but not nearly as poor as the Petersons. "Nobody else I knew," she said, "was *that* poor."

But poverty didn't stop the Petersons from building an active and happy family life. As Oscar's older sister, Daisy, said, "We kids didn't realize we were poor." What gave stability to the Peterson family was the strong commitment they made to their neighborhood. "Everyone knew everyone in the community," Daisy said, "and everyone felt responsible for one another."

For Olivia, a deeply religious woman, the most important connection was to the nearby Union United Church. She made sure all five kids got plenty of exposure to religion. They went to church every Sunday morning, came home for lunch, then returned to the church for Sunday school in the afternoon. They took part in church picnics in the summer and in church concerts year-round. In Oscar's view, Union United was a place where he and his siblings formed ideas about faith and God that they never lost.

The kids' crowded Sundays continued after Sunday school with meetings at 4:30 p.m. of the Universal Negro Improvement Association. The meetings took place in the association's own small and rickety building. All the Petersons attended to hear speakers from the United States, Britain, and the Caribbean Islands, who came to address Canadian organizations like UNIA.

Their subject was always the same: how black people in North America could lift themselves up in a world where whites were the bosses. Some speakers advocated a return of North American blacks to Africa. But most talked about the need for black citizens to push for equality with the dominant white culture and to win the same financial and social rewards.

The Peterson kids soaked up the speakers' messages, and between speeches, they joined the band that presented the musical part of each UNIA meeting. While piano was the main instrument for all the Petersons, as youngsters they learned to play brass instruments. These instruments were borrowed from the Negro Community Center, another organization for the black residents of St. Henri. Along with instruments, the center arranged for older musicians to give free music lessons to the children. Daisy learned to play trombone, and all of the Peterson boys took up either cornet or trumpet. By the very young age of five, Oscar was well launched on the cornet. The kids joined other musicians, both child and adult, in the band that played at UNIA meetings as soon as they developed ease with their instruments.

"The band was a mishmash of instruments – violins, a tuba, my trombone, Oscar's cornet," Daisy remembered. "We played short classical pieces and band music that everybody seemed to like. It was part of life in our community."

But for all the pleasure the brass instruments brought the Petersons, it was the piano they loved most of all.

Even when Daniel Peterson was deep in the worst of his cash shortages, he made sure to keep aside enough to make two monthly payments. One was for the rent on the family house; the other was to lease an old black upright piano.

Daniel's love affair with music began in his years at sea. He had no musical training during his childhood, but as a seaman, he began to learn about music on his own. He started by buying a miniature organ, which folded into the size of a large suitcase. Daniel lugged the little organ on all his travels, teaching himself to work its keyboard in his spare time aboard ship.

At ports along the way, he shopped for sheet music and practice guides. Daniel learned how to read music and how to give the right sounds to the notes on the page. For him, music meant hymns and the classics. There would be no wasting time on popular tunes or frivolous styles. Daniel Peterson's one-man, self-help guide to music was a serious business.

For his family of five children, Daniel worked out a musical plan. All would learn to play the piano. Since he was away on trains for more than half the time, Daniel put together a system to make sure the kids worked on their piano lessons during his long absences.

Under Daniel's system, he taught the piano's basics to his kids when each was just three or four years old. From then on, he assigned the older kids to monitor the younger ones. Once Fred and Daisy understood their father's lessons, they would pass on what they learned to Chuck, Oscar, and May. Everybody chipped in on the learning process, and each child was allowed equal practice time on the old black upright piano after school and on weekends.

Before Daniel left on his trips, he gave every kid a specific piano piece or exercise or scale to learn. When he returned home, he tested the children, making sure they had kept to their assignments. The kids who passed Daniel's test got a small nod of approval. There were no kisses or hugs, just a nod. If a child failed, if Daniel decided the kid hadn't practiced enough, Daniel hauled out a belt and gave him or her a spanking.

Daniel was a stern piano teacher. Though he told his friends how proud he was of the children's talents, he rarely let the kids know his feelings. He wasn't a demonstrative man, and when he was home from his grueling trips, he liked nothing more than the simple pleasure of smoking his cigar and reading his newspaper. But as the overseer of his children's music studies, he showed the demanding side of his personality. He could be a scary father with a belt in his hand.

In the early 1940s, Oscar and his musical family posed for a photographer from his father's employer, the Canadian Pacific Railway. From left to right: Oscar's brother Chuck, wearing his army uniform and holding his trumpet; Oscar on the piano stool; behind him, his father, Daniel; his mother, Olivia; and his two sisters, May and Daisy.

Fred, the eldest child, got Daniel's grand musical plan started on an optimistic note. Fred had a great touch on the piano and moved his hands around the keyboard as if he were born to the instrument. He absorbed his father's lessons in the piano's basics, mastering scales and learning to play the hymns and simple classical pieces.

Though Fred did his duty in helping to teach the other kids, teaching wasn't the part of his father's plan that he was keen on. He often got impatient showing his younger brothers and sisters something that came so easily to him. Fortunately, his reluctance to teach turned out not to be much of a problem because Daisy, younger than Fred by a year, found teaching a pleasure. Daisy freed Fred to go his own way on the piano.

In his early teens, Fred even ventured into popular music, playing the hit tunes of the day and giving them his own variations. That didn't go down well with his father, but Fred's adventures on the keyboard provided the very young Oscar with his first taste of jazz.

In the early 1930s, Fred became seriously ill. He had tuberculosis, an infectious disease that attacked the lungs. TB, which has today been largely wiped out by inoculations in all but the world's poorest countries, was common in North America in the 1920s and '30s. Many sufferers became crippled, while others died.

TB made a terrifying invasion of the Peterson household. Along with Fred, both Daisy and Oscar were diagnosed with the disease. Little Oscar, just eight years old, was taken to Montreal's Children's Memorial Hospital, where he was kept for thirteen months. Simple bed rest was the cure most often prescribed for tuberculosis, and it worked for Oscar.

Slowly he regained his health, but for more than a year, he was away from his family and his piano. In later years, Oscar spoke positively of his experience, remembering the nurses on his hospital ward who made him a favorite, giving him extra hot chocolate and cookies. But there was no telling what long-term damage the disease may have done to his immune system. For much of Oscar's adult life, he suffered from far more than his share of major ailments.

Whatever the results, Oscar never complained about his long stay at the Children's Memorial Hospital. But, then, he rarely complained about much.

Like Oscar, Daisy recovered from her tuberculosis with hospital rest. Fred was not so lucky. Either his TB was more advanced than that of his younger sister and brother or his system was less able to resist the disease. He grew sicker, and in 1934, Fred died. He was just fifteen years old.

Daisy, the second oldest, was the most conscientious of the Peterson kids. She practiced the longest and hardest on the piano. Oscar always said it was Daisy who set the example of dedication. But in Daisy's own case, she may have been too anxious to do well. When she played for her father, anxiety led to nervousness, and she made mistakes. Poor Daisy got more spankings from the belt than any of the other kids.

One day, Daniel invited a few friends to the house to listen to piano recitals by the children, something he often did. Before the guests arrived, Daniel warned Daisy, "Now remember, no mistakes." Daisy reacted by making errors at the beginning of her piece and never recovered, fumbling even more before she reached the finish.

"From that time on," Daisy said, "if I had to play, I was a bundle of nerves. I never enjoyed playing in public again."

Instead of becoming a performer, Daisy developed into a superb piano teacher. She began by instructing children in her own neighborhood, then expanded her range to cover students of all ages from every part of Montreal. To increase her knowledge, she earned a music degree from McGill University, supporting herself for years by working in her mother's occupation as a maid.

In the 1960s, devoted full-time to music, Daisy gained a reputation as perhaps Montreal's most successful all-round piano teacher. Respect for her spread so widely that in 1988, Laurentian University in Sudbury, Ontario, awarded her an honorary doctorate.

Chuck, the third born, was the good-natured kid who loved to joke around. But he was as serious as any of the Petersons about his music. He worked hard at the piano lessons, and he took up trumpet as a second instrument. When the Second World War came along in 1939, Chuck joined the Canadian Army. A military band scooped him up to play in its brass section for marches, parades, and concerts. Chuck never went overseas, remaining in Canada with the band for the entire war.

After peace came in 1945, he set his heart on a career as a featured pianist. He played in a dance band, and while he waited for a chance at his dream to work as a soloist, he took a day job in an aluminum factory. There, the bosses assigned him to operate a press that flattened aluminum plates.

One day, the press jammed to a stop. Chuck reached his left hand into the machine to brush aside whatever was causing the problem. The press came to life so suddenly that Chuck had no chance to pull back his arm. It was crushed, from his elbow to the tips of his fingers.

———

Chuck tried to stay the laughing guy he'd always been, but bitterness gradually seeped into his spirit. By default, since a one-armed man couldn't play the piano but could still blow a wind instrument, he settled for second best, working in the brass sections of dance bands around Montreal. He kept going, relying on ordinary day jobs to pay the bills. But bad luck wasn't finished with poor Chuck.

He suffered from high blood pressure (another health problem that affected several Petersons, including Oscar), emphysema, and kidney failure. His kidney condition worsened in the early 1980s, and in 1983, he checked into the Royal Victoria Hospital.

A friend named Oliver Jones was the last person, apart from the Peterson family, to visit Chuck at the Royal Victoria. Oliver had grown up a few doors away from the Peterson house. As a little boy of five or six, he used to sit on their front steps listening to Oscar, who was nine years older, as Oscar played the piano inside.

Oliver thought it was the most marvelous sound he had ever heard. He took lessons from Daisy Peterson, and over the years, made a scintillating career as a jazz pianist. It was the kind of life that Chuck had once imagined for himself.

In the hospital room, Oliver tried to comfort his old friend Chuck, who seemed beyond consolation.

"I'm sick, and I lost my arm," Chuck said to Oliver. "I never had any luck."

Not long after Oliver's visit, in early 1984, Chuck Peterson died.

———

May was the fifth and youngest child, the one who sometimes seemed the kid left behind. Like her older brothers and sister, she took piano lessons, with Daisy as her first instructor. May developed her talents diligently and became a teacher, launching the musical lives of many of Montreal's children.

But she devoted much of her time from the 1950s to the 1970s taking care of her parents, Olivia and Daniel, at the old family home. In later years, May went to work for Oscar. She organized her brother's schedule, paid his bills, handled his mail, and generally kept his working life in order. As much in love with music as all the other Petersons, May still found time to play her piano.

When Oscar and his brothers and sisters were still young and living at home, everyone in the family recognized that Oscar's gifts put him several steps ahead of the others. Oscar was born with perfect pitch – the ability to identify any note the moment someone played it on the piano. He was the Peterson kid with the infallible musical memory. After one of the other Petersons played through a whole piece, Oscar could sit down at the piano, without a sheet of music in front of him, and repeat the piece note for note.

Once, when Oscar was eleven years old, Daniel instructed both him and Daisy to learn a complicated piano concerto while Daniel was away. Daisy practiced the concerto day and night. Oscar read comic books. But when Daniel returned, Daisy made her usual nervous mistakes while Oscar played the concerto without missing a note. It was all so casual and natural for Oscar.

———

In Oscar's preadolescent years, he began to realize that the music everybody called jazz had captured his imagination above all other categories. He listened to all the jazz he could find on the radio. Not long after his twelfth birthday, he heard his first jazz pianist in person — a West Indian sailor who dropped by the Peterson house to visit his old friend Daniel. Invited by Daniel to sit at the Peterson piano, the sailor proceeded to rip off a few choruses of a tune in a jazz style.

Oscar listened with wonder. When the sailor finished, Oscar promised himself that he would figure out how to play the tune the way the sailor played it — except he would play it even better. He worked hard to get the song exactly where he wanted it. Then he moved on to three or four other tunes that he played over and over, in a treatment he thought of as jazz. As young as Oscar was, he felt the irresistible urge to become a jazz pianist.

But young Oscar had important questions: What was jazz? Where had it come from? And how could he uncover its mysteries?

CHAPTER THREE

THE STORY OF JAZZ

Jazz was born in the American city of New Orleans, Louisiana, in the early years of the twentieth century. The black musicians who played the first jazz worked in the city's nightclubs and speakeasies, where the customers went looking for good times. The people in the clubs wanted music that matched their moods: upbeat in the early evening, slow and blue in the later hours. The musicians set out to give the customers what they asked for.

For inspiration, these early jazzmen turned to the soulful spirituals and down-home blues of America's Deep South. They looked to the high-stepping excitement of the city's marching bands and to the low-down flavor of the popular songs of the day. From all of these sources, the musicians put together something new and shiny. Trained in European classical traditions, many had the skills to rework the familiar music from black people's lives into distinctive and ingratiating sounds and rhythms.

The melodies the jazzmen produced had a vocal feel, as if the men were singing into their trumpets and clarinets and trombones. They matched the melodies to beats and meters that seemed unlike anything the listeners had heard before. The rhythms weren't thick and stolid in the way of marches and hymns. Jazz rhythms were much looser, full of accents that were out of the ordinary. Jazz musicians placed a heavy beat in places where everybody expected a weak beat and a weak beat where a heavy beat usually went.

Jazz broke conventional music's rules, but somehow it evolved as a new form all its own. First called ragtime by the musicians, then jass, and finally jazz, the music was fresh and novel, never failing to surprise its listeners.

Early New Orleans jazz gave the world many fine musicians and one genius. The genius was Louis Armstrong, who played the trumpet and sang. He did everything in a fashion that inspired countless musicians to play like him. They were so taken with Louis that they even dressed in his sharp style. He became every beginning jazzman's idol.

Louis Armstrong, jazz's first great soloist, spent his performing life in the spotlight, enchanting audiences with his powerful trumpet solos and his growly vocals.

Blowing his trumpet with enormous energy and strength, Armstrong got a sound that was large and sumptuous. And on everything he played, he swung. "Swing" was what jazz musicians came to call the rhythm they gave to their music. When Armstrong hit a beat, putting a small shimmy into it, he was swinging. Listeners just couldn't help tapping their feet to the rhythm.

Swing was crucial to jazz, and so was improvisation. Jazz musicians learned to develop their own variations on original melodies. Right there on the bandstands, they dreamed up new musical phrases based on the chords and melodies that the songwriters had put on paper. It was an approach to music that made jazz spontaneous, mysterious, and full of the unexpected.

As in just about everything else in jazz, Louis Armstrong led the way with his talent for embellishment. His trumpet solos soared and swooped. He wasn't as daring in his improvisations as some later players, but the purity in his playing helped make him the ideal jazz musician.

In personality, Armstrong was sunny. Audiences recognized his optimistic nature when they heard him play and sing. He was a showman. When he smiled, it was as if a thousand-watt lightbulb had been turned on. His singing, with the intentionally slurred words and growling diction, was too infectious to resist. And he added showbiz thrills to his jazz. In his prime, he finished each night's performance with a song called "Shine," during which he blew a sensational 250 consecutive high Cs (the musicians in his band kept count).

In the years just before and after 1920, New Orleans musicians spread across the country, carrying jazz in all directions, particularly to America's northern cities.

A five-man group called the Original Dixieland Jazz Band was the first to head north. Traveling from Louisiana to New York City in 1917, the ODJB scored a big hit with Manhattan audiences. It was a triumph that puzzled other New Orleans musicians for two reasons — the first, that the members of the ODJB were white; the second, that their playing amounted to a feeble imitation of the jazz that the pioneering black musicians played with much more creativity.

The black jazzmen couldn't help thinking that if northern audiences were impressed by the music of the ODJB's white players, they'd be knocked out by the real thing from New Orleans's black players. In no time, the black musicians pointed their own way north.

Many of them had already spent years working on riverboats, running up and down the Mississippi from New Orleans as far into the interior as St. Louis, Missouri, and Davenport, Iowa. They presented jazz as the featured onboard entertainment, and it didn't take the musicians long to press further north, close to the top of the Mississippi River. Most of them settled in Chicago, where the rambunctious nightclub scene made a welcoming home for jazz.

Louis Armstrong, who played regularly in riverboat bands, put down roots in Chicago in 1922. "Pops," the other musicians called him. He was jazz's father figure, the man who inspired northern musicians, both black and white, to play jazz. Brilliant new soloists emerged among the younger musicians up north, gathering jazz critical praise and a wider audience.

By the late 1920s, jazz musicians were finding jobs in the big bands that became the major force in popular music for the next three decades. There were two kinds of big bands: sweet and swing. Sweet bands played just for dancing. Swing bands were for listening, though fans who happened to be great at jitterbugging – a frantic and athletic dance style – couldn't resist dancing to the high-powered swing bands.

Swing bands, made up of a dozen to twenty musicians, hit the road throughout North America on long strings of one-nighters in dance halls and pavilions. Each band included at least two or three exceptional jazz soloists, who helped give the bands their distinctive appeal.

Benny Goodman's band led the way in swing popularity. Goodman was white, a clarinet player, and a native of Chicago, where he learned his jazz from the transplanted New Orleans musicians. Besides playing exquisite clarinet solos and leading an exciting big band, Goodman took an adventurous approach to the music business. He was the first band leader to expand jazz's respectability by playing a 1938 concert in Carnegie Hall. And he was the first prominent white leader to hire black musicians for his otherwise all-white band at a time in American music when the races rarely mixed.

The sophisticated Duke Ellington was jazz's most complete composer and arranger, writing every form of music for his band, from pop songs to religious oratorios.

For the most part, big bands made up of black musicians surpassed white bands in jazz skills. No band swung with as much power and finesse as Count Basie's. Jimmie Lunceford's was tops in the precision of its ensemble playing. And for innovations and fresh ideas in big band music, Duke Ellington's band towered above all others.

Ellington, a pianist (as were Basie and Lunceford) and a prolific composer, always said his real instrument was his band. His point was that he shaped his hundreds of compositions around the characteristic sounds and abilities of the band's musicians. His principal players stayed with him for as long as forty years. The pieces Ellington wrote for them included every form, from popular songs to religious oratorios and extended concertos. His body of work made Duke Ellington jazz's most accomplished composer and arranger, a figure as essential to the music and its history as Louis Armstrong.

In the mid-1940s, an alto saxophonist from Kansas City named Charlie Parker, who served his apprenticeships in black big bands, set off a jazz revolution. The trumpeter Dizzy Gillespie once said, "Charlie Parker turned everything upside down." Parker was joined by Gillespie and a handful of other musicians who were having mutinous thoughts about jazz. Together they launched an attack on the music's rhythms, harmonies, and melodies. Their refashioned version of modern jazz, which came to be called bebop, upset jazz's accepted systems.

Bebop melodies were quick and intricate, rather than measured and coherent in the customary jazz style. Where previous jazz rhythms kept mostly to a regular four beats to the bar, the new jazz experimented with all kinds of beats.

It demanded tricky interplay between the bass and the drums, the two instruments that were responsible for pushing the rhythm. Bebop managed one more far-reaching revolution: It broadened jazz's harmonies to produce sounds that were daring and unorthodox.

The masters of the modern form of jazz called bebop performed in concert at Toronto's Massey Hall on May 15, 1953. From left to right: Bud Powell (piano), Charles Mingus (bass), Max Roach (drums), Dizzy Gillespie (trumpet), and Charlie Parker (alto saxophone). The recording of the concert was titled *The Greatest Jazz Concert Ever*.

Young musicians new to jazz fell eagerly into line behind Parker, embracing his music with such fervor that bebop became a kind of underground social movement. Bop musicians and their fans grew little tufts of hair under their lower lip as an identifying sign; they wore sunglasses at all hours of the day and night; and they introduced "cool" as an adjective of approval. It was "hip," another adjective the boppers coined, to play and listen to their music.

Jazz clubs became places where small groups – bop tended to be a form for quartets and quintets – played skittery melodies and jagged rhythms. The music had a nervous excitement, and young jazzmen in the late 1940s couldn't resist the new music's lure. It was bebop's time to shine.

In 1945, the year when Parker, Gillespie, and their fellow pioneers led the bebop charge, Oscar Peterson turned twenty. At a time when most jazz pianists his age were embracing bop, Oscar was an exception. While he made good use of the new music's rhythms and harmonies, he in no way jumped on the bop band-wagon. He had different intuitions about jazz.

From the time he was twelve, eight years earlier, he had been absorbing the established jazz styles. Unconsciously, he'd put himself on a path to become a rounded and versatile pianist, someone who could handle all the styles that other musicians threw his way. He wasn't going to be swept up by a single form, whether it was bebop or anything else. Oscar was determined to come as close as he could get to a complete jazz player.

CHAPTER FOUR

TWO TEACHERS AND THE TEACHERS' PET

L ou Hooper, the man who was destined to become Oscar's first piano teacher – apart from his father and sister Daisy – was born in 1894 in the tiny village of North Buxton, in southwestern Ontario. He remained a Canadian citizen for the rest of his long life, but at age three, his family moved across the American border to Michigan. Musically gifted, young Hooper earned a degree at the Detroit Conservatory of Music and studied for two more years at Columbia University in New York City.

With ambitions to make his living in classical music, he soon discovered that the color bar was set too high in the United States to permit many black men like him into the classical world. Fortunately for Hooper, he was equally at home with jazz, so he decided to divide his time between the two forms of music.

"The truth is," Hooper wrote in his unpublished autobiography, "there is beauty on both sides of the musical fence, jazz and classical."

In 1922, he toured as the accompanist to the great black American concert singer Paul Robeson. But Hooper worked for most of the decade in New York City's Harlem neighborhood. He made his reputation as the ideal pianist in small jazz groups and in the backup bands for such magnificent blues singers as Bessie Smith and Ma Rainey.

Harlem in the 1920s became a place and time when pianists had their day at the top of the jazz heap. The approach to jazz of such forceful players as Fats Waller and Willie the Lion Smith came to be called stride. In the left hand, stride pianists alternated chords and single notes, whipping the hand between the thick chords and the sharply struck single notes with tremendous speed and energy. With the right hand, while the left kept to a mighty jazz beat, they tossed out all kinds of melodic ideas, some of them taken from classical pieces. Like Lou Hooper, many stride pianists had conservatory training.

Hooper's version of stride tended to be understated. By nature, he was dignified and proper, and his playing reflected those qualities. He wasn't showy, but thorough and exact. He could handle all piano roles, able to provide sympathetic accompaniment or step out on his own as a featured soloist.

Lou Hooper, Oscar's first piano teacher outside of the Peterson family, always kept himself looking smart and elegant, as this photograph from the mid-1970s illustrates.

When hard economic times hit North America in the early 1930s, Hooper moved back to Canada, eventually choosing Montreal as home. Once settled there, he reinvented himself as an active all-rounder in the city's music scene. He played in dance bands, organized and conducted a men's choir, and gave piano lessons.

It was Hooper's classical background that made him appealing to Daniel Peterson as a teacher for Oscar. That wasn't why Oscar went along with the choice: He was keen to hear what Mr. Hooper had to tell him about jazz.

At 4:00 p.m. on a Thursday in early 1937, Hooper arrived at the Peterson house for the first lesson. He began by running Oscar through piano exercises. Then Hooper asked Oscar to pick a short classical piece and play it. Oscar chose something by nineteenth-century Polish composer and pianist Frederic Chopin.

When Oscar finished, Hooper slid onto the piano seat and repeated the piece in his own interpretation. "You know, Oscar," Hooper said as he played, "I've always felt that Chopin was looking at a lovely landscape at the time he composed this piece because everything about it is so lush."

At many of the following lessons – every other Thursday afternoon for the next several months – Hooper went through the same drill. As he played short classical pieces, he'd describe the mood of the music, telling Oscar what he thought the composer might have had in mind.

One afternoon, playing a composition by Franz Liszt – the Hungarian pianist and composer of the same general period as Chopin – Hooper said, "Liszt must have been feeling his own strength at this point because as we play it, we can almost feel the transmission of power from his music to us."

Oscar understood the point Mr. Hooper was making. Music wasn't just a matter of notes on a page. Those notes could express emotions, and it was the pianist's job to find those emotions and give them life. Oscar followed Mr. Hooper's other point, too, that Chopin's music was romantic, touched with a bit of melancholy. And Liszt was powerful, confident, and attacking.

Oscar grasped the distinctions. He decided that if he had to make a choice between Chopin and Liszt, he would take Liszt any day. Oscar liked the powerful emotions in Liszt's music: They were what he wanted to produce on the piano himself.

After a few weeks of lessons, Oscar brought up the subject of jazz. In reply, Mr. Hooper said he would play a jazz tune, then Oscar could play one of his own. Mr. Hooper's choice was a ballad, which he played in a clear and gentle style. He included a few bars of his low-key stride phrases, and when he finished, Oscar thought that the song had been lovelier than he could have imagined possible. He made a particular note for his own future reference of the stride passages. And Oscar grew to love a little stride in his own performances.

When Oscar played his jazz piece that afternoon, he was in an exuberant mood. He poured everything into the composition, hitting the keys with force and hard swing. He felt pleased with himself, knowing that his technique and musicianship had been as solid as he could make them.

But when he turned to Mr. Hooper, hoping for praise, all Oscar's teacher said was, "Interesting, Oscar. Very interesting."

Hooper gave lessons to Oscar for several more Thursdays. He often talked about jazz, providing Oscar with hints of what was needed for a pianist to make a life in jazz. Each time, he asked Oscar to play certain pieces, giving his young pupil ideas about ways to adjust his approach but not offering many specific comments about his overall playing.

Then, abruptly, Mr. Hooper told Daniel Peterson that he would no longer be calling on the Peterson house. It was time to leave. He had taken Oscar as far as he could.

Many years later, in Hooper's unpublished autobiography, he explained his reasoning behind the lessons he gave Oscar and the mysterious way he ended them. He said that he recognized Oscar's immense talent from the first piece Oscar ever played for him. Astonished at the twelve-year-old prodigy's amazing gifts, he formed a teaching strategy to deal with them.

"I selected only such musical pieces that would challenge to the utmost his musicianship," Hooper wrote. "As I observed the results through biweekly visits to his home, I was satisfied that this practice was proving satisfactory. It freed Oscar to forge his own illustrious way."

As for Oscar, he honored the musical debt he owed Lou Hooper for the rest of his career.

"He brought into my life a newfound understanding of how best to interpret a musical selection," Oscar wrote. "What he also made me much more aware of was the delicacy and beauty of the piano itself."

In Oscar's everyday teenage life, he was polite, punctual, and respectful of his elders. He said in later years that most kids like him from West Indian backgrounds had good manners drilled into them at home. Certainly Daniel and Olivia Peterson insisted that all their children behave properly, both at school and out in the world, and that they do nothing to bring shame on the Peterson name. Oscar got the message. Not once did he bring home a note from a teacher reporting a single piece of misconduct.

There was only one upsetting episode in high school. It came on his very first day at Montreal High. When he got dressed in the morning, he found that the only pair of pants he could wear had to be patched with pieces of cloth to cover the rips and tears.

Oscar hated going to his new high school looking "like a ragged hobo." But he went, feeling poor, deprived, and, worst of all, humiliated. It was probably no coincidence that, in later years, Oscar was noted for his snazzy clothes. During the rest of his time in high school, he managed to round up the money to dress in neat jackets, ties, and trousers. He never wanted to experience again the mortification of that first day at Montreal High.

Oscar didn't take part in high-school activities unless they involved music. He passed up on sports, clubs, and the annual school play. If he felt he was missing out on normal teenage activities, he never complained. He didn't appear to even notice it: Music ate up all of his time. He was so committed to the piano that he told the rest of his family he was going to become the best jazz pianist in the world.

Daisy, five years older than Oscar, nagged her brother to work hard on the classical side of his piano repertoire. She said that no matter what kind of music Oscar eventually made his living at – jazz or anything else – the classical background would help his technique and his all-round musical knowledge. Oscar agreed.

Daisy took Oscar along with her the day she tried out for a place at Montreal's conservatory of music. She persuaded her thirteen-year-old brother to audition too. Oscar agreed, but he stumbled through the classical number he was asked to play, which didn't impress the judges. But their eyes opened wide in astonishment when Oscar whipped through a piece of George Gershwin jazz and when he demonstrated his perfect pitch.

The conservatory admitted Oscar, but turned away poor Daisy, who once again endured a bout of nerves during her audition. Daisy had wanted desperately to get into the conservatory, but her confidence was just sufficiently off to keep her from performing at her best. Oscar, indifferent to the whole process, won the spot.

In the end, Oscar and the conservatory realized they weren't made for one another. No teacher there made a lasting impression on him, and he dropped out after only a few weeks. It wasn't that Oscar disliked classical music — it was that he simply loved jazz far more.

A few years later, Daisy led Oscar to the man who would become his second significant teacher. Daisy was twenty, and she felt certain that the piano teacher she was seeing for lessons would make a good fit with fifteen-year-old Oscar. The teacher's name was Paul de Marky.

De Marky was much more than a piano teacher. When Daisy took Oscar to meet him, de Marky had been Canada's preeminent classical pianist for many years. Born in Hungary in 1897, he studied piano in Budapest until he immigrated to Canada in 1921. Besides launching a successful solo career from his new home base of Montreal and performing all over the world, he taught at McGill University's Faculty of Music. He also took a few private pupils, making sure they measured up to his high standards. In de Marky's opinion, Daisy measured up. Oscar did, too.

Hungarian Franz Liszt was famous in the nineteenth century as a gifted composer and conductor, but he was even more celebrated for the power and passion of his piano playing.

Since young Oscar was attracted to the music and style of Franz Liszt, he was in the right hands with Paul de Marky. In Budapest, de Marky had studied with a well-known teacher named Stefan Thoman. When Thoman was young, he'd taken lessons from none other than Liszt himself.

The Liszt style was in the bravura tradition of the arts. That meant his playing and his compositions emphasized extravagant qualities – it was a showoff approach to music, full of grand emotions. Liszt wrote, "Music presents at once the intensity and the expression of feeling." In Liszt's playing and in that of people influenced by him, the emotions in the music were out-front and irresistible.

Each Thursday afternoon for almost a year, at a hefty price of fifteen dollars per hour (Daniel Peterson dug deep into his pockets to cover the fee), Oscar studied with de Marky at his studio. Oscar was pleased to discover two things about his new teacher. The first was that this great classical pianist had a firm understanding of jazz piano. At the end of every lesson, de Marky said to Oscar, "All right, now play me what you're doing with your jazz things." Without hesitation, Oscar charged into a tune he'd been working on, something with lots of swing and impro-visation. As the last note died away, de Marky clapped and cheered. Oscar glowed. The Hungarian classical virtuoso was, deep down, a jazz fan who couldn't resist the music.

The second thing about de Marky that pleased Oscar was that he made an immediate connection between Oscar and Liszt. De Marky thought that just as the mature Liszt had reflected large feelings in his classical playing, so did teenaged Oscar in his jazz playing. What Oscar now needed was the right physical training to enable him to play the ideas he formed in his head and the emotions he felt in his heart.

De Marky created fiendishly difficult exercises that emphasized swift and clear note-striking. The idea was to give Oscar something de Marky called speedy fingers. He drilled into Oscar the need to place his hands in exactly the right positions to move around the keyboard with top velocity and efficiency.

Oscar gobbled up de Marky's instruction, working as hard as he ever had during the lessons from the famous concert pianist.

Many years later, Oscar said of de Marky: "He showed me the capacity for portraying on the piano every possible emotion from utter joy to abysmal sadness."

Then, as Lou Hooper had done before him, de Marky told Oscar he had taken him as far as he could. He ended the lessons, sending Oscar off to make his name in the world of jazz pianists. Oscar never again took formal instruction from a trained teacher. And although he picked up ideas from many musicians and incorporated them into his work, for the most part, Oscar was on his own. He liked it that way.

CHAPTER FIVE

THE MOST FAMOUS PIANIST IN CANADA

ne day in 1940, the year Oscar turned fifteen and took lessons from Paul de Marky, Daisy asked him to come with her for a walk.

"Where to?" Oscar asked.

"Never mind," Daisy said.

Even though Oscar was a big kid, imposing for his age, he was still a shy adolescent. Daisy was certain that if she let him know in advance where they were headed, he'd refuse to go.

After twenty minutes, they reached CBM, the local CBC radio station in downtown Montreal. Daisy told Oscar she wanted him to audition for a program. By entering the station, she knew it was too late for Oscar to leave without looking like a coward.

A well-known broadcaster named Ken Soble was running a Canada-wide amateur music contest on CBC Radio. The program was roughly the 1940s radio equivalent of the much later *Canadian Idol* on television. Little-known singers and musicians competed against one another on air, and votes from listeners decided the winner.

On this day, Ken Soble was auditioning people who were keen to take part in the Montreal end of the contest.

Waiting in the studio for his turn, Oscar was nervous. He stepped up to the piano. As soon as he started to play, his nerves steadied. The tune he chose had a lot of flash. Jumping into it, he gave the number all the technique Paul de Marky had taught him.

Soble's reaction was instant. He had no doubt this astounding teenaged pianist would make a fantastic contestant. Oscar passed the audition, and Soble picked him as one of the performers. Through the following weeks of on-air competition, Oscar emerged as the overall Montreal winner.

The victory qualified him for a trip to Toronto, where the contest finals took place. Now he was up against the best of the musicians and singers from the rest of Canada. Oscar may have been a kid up against much older adult musicians, but he was confident. He liked this taste of the limelight.

On air in the Toronto competition, Oscar's performance was dynamic. (Not only was he a rare teenager in the competition, he was a rare black performer.) The combination of his youth and fabulous technique bowled over the radio listeners. Amazed as Ken Soble had been in Montreal, they voted for Oscar in huge numbers. Young Oscar Peterson finished first in the nation-wide contest.

As a prize, the CBC presented him with a check for $250.00, a big sum in those days. It was the first money Oscar earned from jazz – the music that would become his life's passion.

Oscar's success in the radio competition won him several guest spots on other radio shows, making him a minor celebrity around Montreal. But Oscar was just a kid, still in his early high-school years, coming out as an exciting teenage piano sensation at Montreal High.

An institution of 2,500 students, including kids from the St. Henri neighborhood, Montreal High had a baby grand piano in its foyer. Every day, Oscar made the baby grand his unofficial noon-hour headquarters. He pounded out boogie-woogie numbers that wowed the kids who flocked around the piano.

Boogie-woogie, a distant and unruly relative of jazz, was a repetitive, rowdy style of playing, full of thumping left-hand chords and bluesy melodies. If boogie-woogie wasn't art, it still stirred audiences, especially when played at the super-fast tempo Oscar gave it. That was the fun part to him – putting on a show for the other kids. And Oscar soon discovered that boogie-woogie was a great way to meet girls.

More serious business was Montreal High's student orchestra, led by a clarinetist named Percy Ferguson, Oscar's senior by a year.

Percy came from a musical family. His mother commuted regularly to Ottawa, where she played violin in the Ottawa Symphony Orchestra. At home, she had a hand in designing a music program for the city's school system.

Percy's father was the principal at Montreal's Aberdeen School. He allowed the Montreal High band, which Percy named the Victory Serenaders, to rehearse after school in Aberdeen's large kindergarten classroom. Percy's only brother, Maynard, was the band's trumpet whiz, a player with phenomenal range. Maynard was a little guy, and when he soloed, he stood on his band chair so that audiences could see who was blowing those blistering high notes. Maynard, who went on to a long career as leader of his own big band, touring the world for decades, was one of the Serenaders' two main soloists. Oscar, the dynamic pianist, was the other.

The Serenaders played for tea dances in the school gym, for school assemblies, for the Montreal High formal, and for enough other jobs to keep them busy on weekends. The band worked from the stock arrangements of popular tunes that were available at music stores. Under Percy Ferguson's crisp leadership, the teenage players put plenty of pep and discipline into music that might have otherwise been pretty ordinary. Maynard Ferguson tore off electrifying high notes, and Oscar ignited audiences with his powerful solos.

Oscar never let up in his drive to expand the reach of his jazz talent. At home or school, when he practiced, his aim was to give his playing some of the style he picked up from American jazz pianists he heard on the radio. Over time, he settled on two piano players who worked their way into his heart and his fingers.

Before Oscar reached his teens, Teddy Wilson's records had caught his attention. Wilson's quicksilver touch and striking improvisations influenced Oscar throughout his early jazz years.

First came Teddy Wilson. Though Wilson grew up in Alabama, he moved to Chicago in the late 1920s, where he fell under the influence of a trail-blazing pianist named Earl Hines. Hines was one of early jazz's most original soloists, on the level of Louis Armstrong, with whom Hines frequently worked and recorded. Hines played complex single-note passages in his right hand and included such a rich and forceful mix of chords with both hands that he sounded like a one-man orchestra.

In Teddy Wilson's playing, he kept to Hines's essence but toned it down. A stylish man with a small mustache and a placid expression, Wilson sounded on the piano the way he looked in person. His style was poised, his piano touch as light as a feather. Oscar, skipping past Hines as an influence, loved everything about Wilson. He set out to incorporate Wilson's sparkling approach into his own playing.

He heard plenty of Wilson on the radio because Teddy was one of two black musicians Benny Goodman took into his band in 1937 (the vibraphonist Lionel Hampton was the other). With Goodman, Wilson didn't perform or record in the full band – that would have been too much black-white integration for America to accept at the time.

Instead, Wilson was featured more cautiously by Goodman as a member of a trio and a quartet drawn from within the band. The trio was made up of Wilson, Goodman, and the band's drummer, Gene Krupa. Lionel Hampton was added for the quartet. Both small groups earned the status of legends among critics, fans, and Oscar Peterson.

Nat Cole was Oscar's other piano hero.

As a kid growing up in Chicago, young Nat used to stand outside the Grand Terrance nightclub, where the Hines band was the feature attraction. Cole soaked up the Hines piano approach. Then, like Wilson, he stripped it down to something simpler, a style with more ease. In Cole's playing, all sense of effort vanished.

Oscar found lots of Cole on the radio, both in recordings and in live appearances by the Nat "King" Cole Trio on a program broadcast every Saturday at dinnertime. In the 1940s, Cole gained a higher profile when he added vocals to his performances. His silky voice and immaculate diction transformed him into a major music star. But it was his piano playing that entranced Oscar.

Most listeners loved Nat Cole for his mellow singing style. But long before the popularity of his vocals, Cole was a superb jazz pianist, often performing with his own trio of piano, bass, and guitar. Cole's effortless piano style worked its magic on Oscar.

When Oscar was thirteen, his father thought the boy might have been getting a little full of himself, thinking he was already a piano whiz – a future Teddy Wilson or Nat Cole. To put Oscar in his place, Daniel sat him down and played a piano recording of "Tiger Rag." The song was taken at an outrageously fast tempo and overflowed with runs, arpeggios, and pianistic ideas, all hurrying one another along.

"Oh, I get it!" Oscar said, after he recovered from the shock of the record. "That's not one piano player! There are *two* pianos on that record!"

"Only one, Oscar," Daniel said. "His name is Art Tatum. You think you can play like that?"

Oscar knew he couldn't. Not yet.

Art Tatum, who was born in 1909 and studied at the School of Music in Toledo, Ohio, was one of a kind. He had no vision in one eye and only ten percent in the other. But all he needed was the feel of a keyboard under his fingers and he was off and flying.

Tatum's stupendous technique surpassed that of just about every other pianist in the world, jazz or classical. Yet his touch was remarkably delicate, and his imagination was wild and unpredictable. In the midst of his embellishments and improvisations, he dropped in humorous asides, took off on joyous flights, and was apt to double the tempo without warning.

Tatum was an artist beyond category – the pianist who set the bar that Oscar hoped to equal.

Art Tatum, sixteen years older than Oscar and almost totally blind, was renowned for his prodigious piano technique. Nobody would rival him for speed and dexterity until Oscar took up the Tatum challenge.

When Oscar was still in his midteens and still at Montreal High, he knew he had outgrown the Victory Serenaders. He would rather play in a more professional big band.

In the 1940s, Montreal's best and busiest big band was the one led by trumpet player Johnny Holmes. Besides playing trumpet, Holmes wrote catchy arrangements of popular songs and jazz standards. He put together his band in 1940, when he was twenty-four, playing on weekends and spending the rest of his time as a salesman for a pharmaceutical company.

Swing fans loved Holmes's arrangements and the band's sophisticated jazz touches. Every Saturday night, Holmes was booked for the popular dances at the Victoria Hall in Westmount. It didn't take long for the Holmes band to become the first choice for organizations and wealthy patrons putting on dance parties at Montreal hotels, especially at the very fashionable Ritz-Carlton on Sherbrooke Street.

Holmes was soon earning enough money from his band to quit the pharmaceutical job. But the band wasn't bringing in quite enough to pay the other musicians a living wage. Unlike Holmes, they needed to keep their day jobs, but in the summers, all band members took their holidays during the same two weeks, which gave them time to tour the dance pavilions in Quebec's and Ontario's cottage country.

Just one obstacle got in the way of Johnny Holmes's complete success. The Second World War was on, and the military kept summoning his musicians into service. In early 1942, the army drafted Holmes's regular piano player, then took the pianist who replaced the regular guy, leaving the band with no one to play. At this critical moment, Oscar Peterson, just seventeen, entered the picture.

The link between the two came by way of Art Morrow, a former Holmes alto saxophonist who had been summoned into the army. Morrow found himself with the same military band in which Oscar's brother Chuck played trumpet. Through Chuck, Morrow visited the Peterson home and heard Oscar at the piano.

Morrow was so dazzled that he rushed Oscar to an audition for the vacant spot in the Holmes band.

A sharp judge of musical talent, Holmes called Oscar "a diamond in the rough." He appreciated Oscar's prodigious technique and recognized with pleasure the influences of Teddy Wilson and Nat Cole. Naturally Holmes was going to hire Oscar, but he knew his new pianist, a boy still in high school, had work to do on his style.

To Holmes's ear, Oscar packed all his ideas for solos into one frantic chorus, an approach that tended to limit Oscar's solo spots. He also thought Oscar was confident at fast tempos, but not so steady on slow ballads. Holmes said Oscar needed to learn about pacing and mood before he could hold his own in the demanding business of big band swing. Holmes appointed himself Oscar's mentor.

Oscar, third from left, spent five years absorbing essential lessons in pacing and improvisation from Johnny Holmes, trumpet player and leader of Montreal's most accomplished big band of the 1940s.

Holmes gave Oscar private sessions at no charge. He taught him how to structure a jazz solo; how to slow down his imagination to accommodate a ballad; how to feel comfortable with the other instruments in the band at any tempo. Oscar got a handle on the Holmes teachings in a hurry. Even so, the lessons continued, with more guidance and subtle suggestions, over the five years that Oscar remained with Holmes.

It was Holmes who got Oscar interested in writing his own tunes. Holmes pointed out that Oscar could use the melodies he created in his improvisations as the basis for entire songs. He showed Oscar how to write out arrangements of these numbers for the whole band to play. These simple lessons got Oscar launched on song-writing, something he continued to work on through his entire career.

During the long tenure with Holmes, Oscar emerged as the band's number-one attraction. Holmes hired plenty of talented musicians – the Ferguson brothers, Percy and Maynard, joined the band for a year – but Oscar was the performer who drew the crowds. Holmes wrote arrangements for tunes that allowed Oscar extra solo time. And for the last fifteen minutes of each night's performance, Holmes showcased Oscar playing dreamy ballads in a display of his blossoming confidence with romantic music.

The fifteen minutes grew into an occasion for the rest of the band to test Oscar. Their game was to call out titles of ballads that Oscar was expected to incorporate in whatever tune he was playing. If his tune was "Body and Soul," someone might shout "I Surrender, Dear," and Oscar would segue seamlessly into the second song.

"The guys called out all kinds of things, classical pieces even," Johnny Holmes said. "Oscar never got hung up once. The band idolized Oscar, and the dancers loved his playing."

Holmes raised Oscar's pay. Before long, he and Holmes were the only two musicians earning a living with the Johnny Holmes Band.

Everybody in Montreal who cared about jazz knew that the intersection of Mountain Street and St. Antoine was nick-named "the Corner." On the east side of Mountain, where it met St. Antoine, stood a nightclub named Rockhead's Paradise. The west side of Mountain was home to another hot night-spot called Café St. Michel. Both clubs made the Corner jump with jazz from early evening until it was time for the sun to come up.

The nightly floor shows in each place featured nonstop entertainment by singers, tap dancers, acrobats, trick roller skaters, comedians, and striptease artistes. Providing the music behind the acts were bands comprised mostly of Montreal's best black jazz musicians. The skaters, dancers, and other performers brought along their own jazz-flavored accompaniments written out in sheet music for the bands to play. Between acts, the bands were turned loose to blow their own hard-swinging numbers. For jazz musicians and fans, the clubs represented a little musical bliss.

Just as the teenaged Nat Cole eavesdropped on the Earl Hines Band in Chicago many years earlier, the teenaged Oscar, whose home was a few blocks from the Corner, soaked up the hot music outside Rockhead's Paradise and Café St. Michel. But Oscar actually got inside the clubs. Aware of his emerging talent, the musicians in Café St. Michel in particular invited him in to absorb the jazz at closer quarters. They even gave him a chance to show his stuff on the piano.

Steep Wade, an intense piano player who loved bebop, took Oscar under his wing. Wade worked mostly at the St. Michel and developed a mentoring friendship with Oscar. Often, in the middle of a number, he motioned Oscar to the bandstand.

"Take it," Wade would say, sliding off the piano bench. "I'll be back later."

Without missing a beat, Oscar filled in for the rest of the band's set.

Wade encouraged Oscar to stick around Café St. Michel after the floor show ended and the customers headed home. In these early hours, the jazz musicians stayed on to jam with one another. They took turns blowing solos, testing, playing every lick they could think of to challenge the next guy on the horn or the piano.

Musicians from other clubs dropped by, players from Rockhead's Paradise across the street and from lesser spots around town. Big-name American musicians often joined in, players who were in Montreal for a date at a concert hall or at one of the bigger clubs. Everyone got into the act. The jazz grew hot, sweaty, and inventive. Oscar, given a chance to sit in, learned lessons in jazz at the feet of some of its masters.

In the autumn of 1943, the year after Oscar started earning fairly serious money from Johnny Holmes, he gathered his courage to approach his father for a heart-to-heart talk. Oscar told Daniel he wanted to leave school. He knew his future lay in music; now he needed to put Montreal High behind him and get started on his life's ambition.

To Oscar's astonishment, his father agreed.

"The only condition is that you don't turn into just any ordinary piano player," Daniel Peterson said. "You have to promise to be the best."

A flabbergasted Oscar agreed. He'd already decided to aim for status on his own. He always said he wanted to be the best in the whole world.

Then Daniel surprised Oscar a second time. When Oscar said he might have a tough time at the start and money would probably be slow in coming in, Daniel waved off Oscar's doubts. Prosperity was certain for a musician as gifted as his boy.

In launching his full-time jazz career, Oscar had the savvy guidance of the generous Johnny Holmes, who became Oscar's business manager. Holmes had a simple plan: First he helped Oscar form a trio – piano, bass, drums – and then he booked the group into small clubs around Quebec.

Oscar's frequent appearances on radio shows around town had already built a "Peterson" audience. Soon Holmes spread Oscar's working life beyond Quebec. In Toronto, Oscar sold out a concert at Massey Hall. He packed a four-thousand-seat arena in Winnipeg and drew good crowds in other western cities. Oscar had become Canada's most popular homegrown jazz pianist.

In early 1945, Oscar made the bold move of phoning a man named Hugh Joseph, who ran RCA Victor. RCA was among the biggest recording companies in Canada. On the phone, Oscar introduced himself and said he wanted to make records. Joseph, who loved Oscar's playing, wasted no time in getting the Peterson name on a contract.

Before the end of the year, RCA Victor issued Oscar's first two records at 78 rpm — the commercial form of the time. And another two dozen Peterson 78s reached the market in the following four years. Both RCA and Oscar told interviewers that the records sold in the thousands. For a jazz pianist, not as easy for a record label to market as a singer or a big band, the numbers were impressive.

To Oscar, there was one downside to the recording part of his career. Almost a third of his 78s, the ones that sold the most copies, featured boogie-woogie. Oscar recorded "The Sheik of Araby," "I Got Rhythm," and other popular standards, giving the well-known songs a boogie-woogie treatment. The gimmicky result was popular with everybody, except hip jazz listeners and Oscar himself. He thought boogie-woogie came nowhere close to reflecting his more sophisticated playing.

Oscar took his complaint to Hugh Joseph.

"Well, you'll have to make up your mind, Oscar," Joseph said. "Do you want to be a good commercial musician, or do you want to be a collector's item?"

"A collector's item!" Oscar answered.

In the end, Oscar didn't entirely take the serious route. He recorded more pure jazz after his conversation with Joseph, but he still cut a share of boogie-woogie sides. Oscar needed the money boogie-woogie brought in. By 1947, he had been a married man with financial responsibilities for almost three years.

Oscar first noticed Lillian Fraser in church. She was a couple of years younger than him, but a mature-looking girl with a pretty face. Oscar later described Lil as "a soft, warm, straight-ahead person." As for Lil, she thought Oscar was the most grown-up teenager she ever expected to meet.

Lil lived in Verdun, a few blocks east of Oscar's neighborhood. She was the oldest of four children, two girls and two boys, and like Daniel Peterson, Lil's father worked as a railroad porter. Her two brothers followed their father into porter jobs.

Both Fraser parents were solid devout people who expected the boy who called on their daughter to be polite and respectful. Though Oscar loved to joke around, he minded his manners with the Fraser family. He arranged for a friend who knew the Frasers to introduce him formally, and every time Oscar took Lil on a date, he arrived at the house with a gift. Oscar had serious intentions.

In September 1944, he and Lil were married at Union United Church in St. Henri. Oscar's brother Chuck stood up for him as his best man, and Lil's sister Joan was her maid of honor. On the day of the ceremony, Oscar was nineteen, Lil seventeen. Both mothers worried that the bride and groom were far too young. But Oscar and Lil didn't doubt that they would have a long life as husband and wife.

"Oscar was still a boy," Lil said, "but he looked and thought like a man."

The Alberta Hotel lay across Peel Street from Windsor Station, Montreal's main train station. The location made the hotel a bustling place, filled with travelers waiting to catch trains in all directions from Montreal.

In the autumn of 1947, the hotel opened a lounge on its ground floor. Named the Alberta Lounge, the room held enough tables and heavy red-leather chairs to seat about one hundred patrons. Against one wall stood a small bandstand, just the right size for a piano trio.

Over the first two years of the lounge's existence, Oscar's small group – billed as the Oscar Peterson Trio and made up of piano, bass, and drums – occupied the stand five nights a week. Oscar and Johnny Holmes recognized that Oscar had long since outgrown both Johnny's big band and playing the small bars around Quebec. The time had come for him to settle down in one place, earn a decent paycheck, and hone his style. While Oscar continued to accept occasional concert dates around the country, the Alberta Lounge became his musical home.

It was the place where Oscar worked and reworked his repertoire, adding elements to his already distinct piano sound. Here he met the man who would steer him into jazz's big time.

CHAPTER SIX

NORMAN TAKES CHARGE

N orman Granz's discovery of Oscar was a story Granz told often and colorfully. He exaggerated some details and left out others to make the story amusing. But in all versions, the action began with a one-day JATP business trip that Granz took to Montreal in the midsummer of 1949.

Winding up things in the city that evening, he hailed a taxi to take him to Dorval Airport. In Granz's version, the cab's radio was broadcasting the music of a jazz pianist. The sound caught Granz's attention.

"Any idea whose record they're playing?" he asked the driver.

"Oscar Peterson," the driver answered. "And it isn't a record."

"Not a record? What do you mean?"

"I mean that's him playing live right now," the driver said. "From the club where he works."

The night Granz was in the cab must have been a Wednesday since it was only on Wednesdays that Montreal radio station CJAD broadcast from the Alberta.

"His name's what, did you say?" Granz asked.

"Oscar Peterson," the driver said. "He's the best in the city. Probably in the country."

"So the club where he's playing, it's here in Montreal?"

"Back downtown," the driver answered. "The Alberta Lounge."

"Turn around," Granz ordered. "Take me to the Alberta."

"What about the airport?"

"Never mind the airport." Granz said. "I want to hear the piano player."

Granz spent the rest of the evening listening to Oscar and convincing him to join JATP at the Carnegie Hall concert that September. By the time Granz once again headed for Dorval Airport, he had set Oscar on a path to great things.

He had also made a small difference in Oscar's repertoire.

"I didn't much like the boogie-woogie you played tonight," Granz said to Oscar at the Alberta.

"Customers ask for it," Oscar replied.

"Well, listen, get rid of the boogie-woogie," Granz said. "You don't need it."

Oscar smiled. He was glad for an excuse to cut back the

boogie-woogie – he was tired of pandering to the boogie-woogie crowd.

On the night Norman Granz entered Oscar's life, Granz was thirty-one years old and had already earned his first million dollars from JATP concerts and recordings. He was tall, slim, a fast talker, with sandy hair and exceptionally bushy eyebrows. Everybody who met Granz remembered the eyebrows, just as they never failed to notice his brown-and-white saddle shoes. The shoes had been part of his wardrobe since college days in his native California.

In the mid-1940s, while he worked in the Los Angeles brokerage business, Granz staged weekly jazz nights at local clubs. He'd loved jazz from the time he was a kid. As an adult, he wanted to get closer to the music. Since he had no playing talent, the role of jazz promoter seemed the next best thing.

Granz also looked on the club nights as his chance to advance civil liberties. He was a liberal in his politics, and if one social condition in America outraged him, it was racial discrimination. Many nightclubs in Los Angeles banned blacks from their premises, but Granz insisted on a clause in his contracts forbidding such segregation.

In the summer of 1944, Granz expanded his jazz business from the small-profit club dates to the more rewarding concert promotion. Operating with three hundred dollars of borrowed money, he set out to put on a show at L.A.'s spacious Philharmonic Auditorium. But when he barely had the promotion under way, he thought a printing error had ruined his chances of success.

In a relationship unique in jazz, Norman Granz managed Oscar's career for most of a half-century. Both men prospered from the long connection.

The printer Granz hired to run off the tickets and advertising circulars couldn't find enough space on the printed material for the full line "Jazz at the Philharmonic Auditorium." Without saying a word to Granz, the printer shortened the line to "Jazz at the Philharmonic."

Granz was furious. He thought nobody would be able to figure out where his jazz concert was taking place. But on concert night, July 2, the Philharmonic Auditorium was packed. The jazz audience had no trouble finding their way to the hall, and they went wild over the music.

Granz was so elated by the first concert that he booked the Philharmonic Auditorium for more shows. When he thought about it, he realized that the bumbling printer had arrived at an ideal title for the concerts. From then on, in whatever venue in whatever city Granz presented his shows, he billed them as "Jazz at the Philharmonic." The name caught on, and the four letters, JATP, were burned into the minds of jazz fans.

Granz arrived at a straightforward formula for the concerts. He rarely booked established groups, but instead went for individual musicians whom he put onstage in seemingly random combinations. Spontaneity was what he was looking for. In style, Granz favored small group swing, though he soon added bebop to the mix. And while his preference was for musicians with name recognition – Nat Cole played at the July 2, 1944, concert – he usually included a few promising younger musicians and one or two overlooked but worthy older players.

Essentially Granz was offering his audiences public versions of the jam sessions that musicians took part in during their private after-hours get-togethers. To bump up the level of excitement, Granz added staged competition among the musicians. Audiences turned out to be as keen on drum battles and trumpet warfare as Granz was. No JATP concert was considered a success unless fans whooped, hollered, and chanted, "Go, go, go!" at the musicians.

Granz recorded the first JATP concerts, and in late 1945, he issued a package of the recordings in an album of 78 rpm discs. The album sold 150,000 copies – an astronomical number for jazz. To Granz, the record sales were the ultimate evidence that he was on to a hot commercial property.

His next step was to book concert tours across the United States, taking JATP national and, if you count the Canadian stops on the Granz schedule, international.

"What I thought I could do," Granz said, "was give the people in Des Moines and El Paso the kind of jazz they'd otherwise never hear."

His thinking proved to be inspired. The concerts, which had drawn such excited audiences in California, stirred the same fervor in cities of all sizes in all parts of the country. Fans everywhere were dying to pay for the chance to hear jazz played by musicians who were, until then, available to them only on records.

For the tours, Granz ran a one-man operation. He chose the musicians; decided on the cities to book for concerts; and organized hotels, meals, and transportation for everyone in his caravan of players. He traveled on the buses and planes with the musicians. As the JATP spokesman, he handled the publicity, gave radio interviews, and talked up the music to the local media at every stop.

In the concert halls on show nights, he micromanaged the details. As well as acting as master of ceremonies, he marshaled the musicians on and off the stage in the order and in the groupings he ordered. For the most part, he ran a tight ship, though the operation wasn't without glitches. Jazz musicians could be casual about timetables and backstage discipline.

"I lost my temper every five minutes," Granz said.

His patience was taxed to the limit by the creative bebopper Charlie Parker, who had become a heroin addict. Parker's addiction made him so unreliable that he often showed up for concerts late or not at all. But Granz never gave up on Parker, booking him year after year. He even covered much of Parker's funeral costs when the heroin killed him at age thirty-four in 1955. Granz could never be faulted for a lack of loyalty to his musicians.

———

Despite obstacles like the Parker episodes, JATP grew into a jazz juggernaut in an astonishingly short period. Before Granz, exhausted by the work, ended the JATP operations in 1959, he had shepherded his musicians on twenty-five tours across North America, Europe, and the Far East. He recorded several of the concerts and bundled them into best-selling albums on the three record labels he founded: Clef, then Norgran, then the immensely profitable Verve.

Adding in the studio recordings that he produced, Granz accumulated a catalogue of more jazz albums than any other single producer. In one typical Granz studio marathon in 1953, he recorded Art Tatum in 124 piano solos. Over time, Granz released the solos in thirteen Tatum albums. Sooner or later, just about everything Granz touched turned to jazz gold.

In the months after Oscar's 1949 Carnegie Hall debut, he and Granz formed a bond that lasted until Granz's death in 2001. What began as a mentoring relationship, with Granz serving as the wise advisor, turned into an enduring friendship. On later JATP tours, the two often roomed together. And on European trips, Oscar was Granz's companion on visits Granz led to art galleries and five-star restaurants.

On the business side, Oscar asked Granz to act as his manager not long after they met. Management was a role that Granz didn't have much taste for. He took on Ella Fitzgerald much later, briefly managed Duke Ellington, and turned down virtually all others wanting him to bail out their disorganized careers.

But with Oscar in 1949, Granz knew he had a star in the making. It helped that Granz happened to be very fond of Oscar. He decided to make an exception to his anti-management rule in Oscar's case. The manager-client deal between the two, never put on paper, was sealed with a handshake. And for most of Oscar's career, it was Granz who booked his concerts and club dates and produced his records.

In the apt phrase of Whitney Balliett, the longtime jazz critic for *The New Yorker* magazine, Granz proceeded to "handmaiden Peterson into fame."

In September 1950, Granz took Oscar on a permanent leap into the big time, signing him for JATP's tenth national tour (Oscar would play in all of JATP's remaining fifteen full tours). Tour number ten began in Hartford, Connecticut, performed in cities in most areas of the country – north, south, east, and west – and finished at Christmastime in Los Angeles. Oscar, on board as the principal piano player for the entire four months, assumed his new position with apprehension.

"I was the kid of the tour, like a rookie starting with the New York Yankees," he recalled. "I had listened to these famous musicians on records for years, and I just didn't know how they'd receive me and how I'd get along with them musically."

Oscar had already proved at his 1949 debut that he measured up to the rest of the JATP cast as a soloist. He felt sure of himself in that role, but he knew the real work would come in filling his other assignment as the tour accompanist. Oscar's task was to back the trumpet players, the tenor saxophonists, and all the other JATP horn players. Despite the nervous doubts he felt at the tour's beginning, Oscar proved to be a quick study.

Among the musicians, one of the three tenor saxophonists

was Lester Young, a musician whose style was the exact opposite of Oscar's. While Young tended to be detached and eloquent in an undemonstrative way, Oscar was bold and energized. As the accompanist, it was up to Oscar to adjust his style to Young's. Not letting his ego get in the way, Oscar went gracefully about the business of reining himself in, allowing Young to tiptoe unhindered into his lovely moments of solo understatement.

When Oscar toured through the 1950s with Norman Granz's troupe, Jazz at the Philharmonic, the most difficult musician for him to accompany was the cool and detached tenor saxophonist Lester Young.

With the other two tenor saxophonists, Illinois Jacquet and Flip Phillips, Oscar was instantly compatible. Both Jacquet and Phillips blew with fat breathy tones and took a rambunctious approach to soloing. When the two pushed one another to raucous charges up and down the keys on their saxophones, Oscar churned away in the background, encouraging even more outrageous excitement.

He was equally sympathetic with the two trumpet players, Roy Eldridge and Dizzy Gillespie. Eldridge played in a style rooted in the swing era. That was right up Oscar's alley. He had grown up with a heavy dose of swing, and Eldridge was his idea of a swing hero. Gillespie was the bebop master, though jazz styles didn't matter to a free spirit like him. He had heard Oscar play a couple of years earlier in Montreal, and back then, Oscar's speed and imagination knocked him out. After the first few nights of the JATP tour, he told anyone who would listen that Oscar was the best pianist he'd ever played with. Years later, Gillespie heaped on more praise, saying Oscar was the best pianist he had ever *heard*.

Oscar began the first JATP tour as the rookie and ended it as the star. His poised and polished solos and his appealing youth made him a hit with the JATP audiences. They went wild for the new piano player. In those moments, Oscar realized that Granz's troupe was exactly the right place for a pianist like him, who had worked for years developing a versatile style built on power and technique. Nowhere else would "the jazz reincarnation of Franz Liszt" – a phrase Oscar's teacher, Paul de Marky, bestowed on him – have flourished so swiftly and extravagantly.

At the end of Oscar's first year of touring, *DownBeat*

magazine's annual readers' poll voted him Best Pianist in 1950. The poll was a reliable measure of a jazz musician's popularity, and Oscar kept on winning. Seventeen times out of the twenty voting years in the 1950s and the 1960s, he was named best among all piano players.

Within not much more than a year of arriving on the American scene, Oscar zoomed to recognition as jazz's number-one pianist. He stayed on top for decades.

Oscar felt proud that he was now earning enough money to make a secure life for his family. He and Lil bought a house in Montreal's Notre-Dame-de-Grâce neighborhood. They lived there until the late 1950s, when Oscar decided they should move to Toronto, which had outdistanced Montreal as the Canadian center for jazz.

Their new home was in suburban Scarborough, a four-bedroom bungalow with a finished basement. It had a recreation room with space for Oscar's precious record collection, a stereo system, and an ebony grand piano that an admirer in Denmark had given him.

Before the move to Toronto, Lil had given birth to children in the same number that Oscar's mother had done decades earlier – at an even faster rate. The first child was Lynn, born in 1948. Sharon came along a year later, and Gay a year after that. Following two years free of new babies, Oscar Junior and Norman were added to the family in next the two years.

Five children in seven years put a heavy burden on a woman as young as Lil. Oscar was at home for the birth of only one of the kids, and he was off on jazz tours for much of normal family time.

Oscar and his first wife, Lil (far right), had five lively kids: Norman, Oscar Junior, Gay, Sharon, and Lynn. But Oscar's family life suffered from his long absences on the road.

Alone in the house, her husband thousands of miles away, Lil needed relief – just some small change in the constant round of childcare. During the two-year gap between the births of Gay and Oscar Junior, Lil suggested to Oscar that she find a part-time job, something to get her out of the house.

"We don't need the money," Oscar answered, ending the discussion.

The feminist movement was years away. The tide would turn when housewives began to demand and win rights in running their own lives. Until that day came, it was common in the 1950s for husbands to make the house rules.

"I get terribly lonely," Lil said in the autumn of 1958. "The nights are the worst. I sit and knit, listen to records, and feel miserably blue."

From the road, Oscar wrote twenty-page letters to Lil, explaining that he, too, experienced unhappiness at their separations. "During my long absences," Oscar admitted, "I felt I had lost my family."

Oscar tried his best. He took Lil with him on one JATP tour to Europe. And often, when he was far away but had a break from work for a day or two, he flew home to see Lil and the kids, even if he could stay only ten or twelve hours before catching a plane back.

No matter how hard Oscar tried, nothing seemed to work in coping with Lil's loneliness. When he came home for longer stretches, friends rushed to their telephones. They wanted the Petersons to go out to dinner, host parties, visit jazz clubs. Oscar didn't mind. A gregarious man, he felt comfortable at small dinner gatherings, telling stories and entertaining his friends.

But that wasn't what Lil expected in her marriage. She was a wife who wanted her husband's company, preferably around the house. It wasn't lost on either Lil or Oscar that she'd probably be happier with a man who had a nine-to-five job than with a largely absent, famous, and accomplished husband.

Oscar knew his marriage was faltering. As if that wasn't tough enough, he found himself up against another problem in his early years of touring. It wasn't entirely new to Oscar, but a problem that, especially in the Deep South region of the United States, brought him heartache he had never before experienced.

CHAPTER SEVEN

RACISM

The first time Oscar's name appeared on the front pages of Canadian newspapers, rather than in the entertainment pages, the story wasn't about his music. It was about a haircut he never got.

The non-haircut took place in early May of 1951, in Hamilton, Ontario. Oscar was booked for a week at a handsome little cocktail bar called the Hunting Room in the downtown Fischer Hotel. Playing in a duo, Oscar was accompanied by the bassist Ray Brown.

Oscar had wanted to work with Brown ever since they played together at Oscar's 1949 Carnegie Hall debut. Brown was a husky man, with a dapper mustache and a mischievous smile. He got an astonishingly big and beautiful sound on the bass, and he had a reliable ear for picking out just the right complementary notes for the pianists he accompanied.

Unfortunately for Oscar, Brown was busy in the late 1940s and early 1950s playing bass in the trio backing his wife, the singer Ella Fitzgerald. With Brown alongside her, the popular Ella toured with JATP and performed in clubs and concerts all over the world. When the marriage began to fall apart — the couple would divorce in 1952 — Brown was free to join Oscar. The two played together for the next seventeen years, at first as a twosome but for far longer as two-thirds of the Oscar Peterson Trio.

In 1951, a black man's first choice to get a haircut in a strange city, usually his only choice, was to find a black barber. Ray Brown, wanting a cut in Hamilton, found no black barbers. When he went into a barbershop near the Fischer Hotel, the white barber's only question was, "How do you want it cut?" Then he trimmed Brown's hair. "Not a bad cut," Brown said afterward.

A day later, when Oscar needed a haircut, Brown steered him to the shop down the street with the accommodating barber. Given Brown's positive recommendation, Oscar was puzzled when he walked into the shop and the barber said abruptly, "We're closed."

Oscar went away, thought about the rude reception, and returned to the shop.

"We're still closed," the barber said.

As Oscar stood at the door, absorbing the second brush-off, a white customer arrived and was shown to a chair.

Feeling angry at what he recognized as racial discrimination, Oscar described his experience to Lloyd Fischer, who owned the Fischer Hotel. An important man around town, Fischer put in two phone calls. One was to the local crown attorney. The other was to the city's major newspaper, the *Spectator*.

The next day, after reporters interviewed Oscar and Ray Brown, the *Spectator* wrote of Oscar's humiliating treatment on the front page. Other newspapers across the country picked up the story.

"When something like this happens," Oscar was quoted in the article, "it almost makes you feel you are not a man."

As the *Spectator* continued to cover the story, and as the other Canadian newspapers repeated the *Spectator's* reporting, a man named Glenn McQuaid tried to explain away the ugly episode. McQuaid owned the Hamilton barbershop. He was the barber who had trimmed Ray Brown's hair, but he wasn't at work on the day Oscar came for a cut. His absence from the shop was the point he wanted to make.

"I'm the only one in the shop qualified to cut a Negro's hair," McQuaid said. "If you don't know how to do it like I do, you would probably break five combs."

Hamilton's mayor apologized to Oscar. Young men from the National Federation of Labor Youth picketed McQuaid's shop, waving signs with angry messages about discrimination. Hamilton's other barbers, pointing out that McQuaid's shop wasn't unionized, blamed Oscar for his own grief: If he had patronized a unionized shop, he would have got his haircut.

McQuaid issued a mild apology to Oscar, though not in person. The Crown Attorney's Office decided to lay no charges. And Oscar told Hamilton's mayor to just forget the whole thing.

But Oscar didn't forget it, nor did he forgive. The hurt ran too deep. The barbershop episode, with its silly talk of his hair breaking combs, could have seemed trivial to white people. But Oscar had to agree with Ray Brown when Brown said, "Oh, man, you tell me there's no discrimination up here in Canada? Yeah? Really?"

Oscar knew about the pain of racial insults. He'd been feeling it all his life.

When he was a boy, white kids called him the N-word. So did his white teacher in grade four. Every time he heard the word, Oscar loathed it and all that it stood for.

As he grew into his teens, he discovered that the hatefulness could reach beyond words. When Oscar joined Johnny Holmes's band, the manager of the Ritz-Carlton hotel told Holmes his band couldn't play there as long as it had a black pianist.

Holmes threatened to run an advertisement in all three Montreal daily papers about the Ritz's racist policy. The manager backed down. Oscar played the Ritz with the band, though once again his pride had taken a blow.

Oscar could never predict when bigotry would come at him. One week, playing the Alberta Lounge, a white patron came to hear his trio several nights in a row. The Alberta's manager introduced Oscar to the enthusiastic fan. For the next ten minutes, the man raved about Oscar's playing.

"With your kind of talent," the man said, speaking in the accent of a man from America's Deep South, "you should come down and share it with us."

Oscar reached out to shake the man's hand in gratitude, but the man pulled away.

"Down home in Georgia," he said, "we don't shake hands with a nigger."

Oscar was stunned.

"It's disorienting, a situation like that," he said later. "You wonder who you really are. Are you a piano player who the other person admires? Or are you just this black man who isn't worth anything, not even a handshake?"

In the fall of 1950, at the time Oscar joined his first JATP tour, Norman Granz suggested that Oscar pass up the weeks when the tour traveled through the southern states.

That year, history was still a dozen years away from the emergence of Martin Luther King Jr. and the turning of the tide in the struggle for civil rights. Segregation of the races remained in place. Granz wasn't sure that Oscar, the young man from Canada who supposedly wasn't exposed to such open racism, would be able to handle the stresses that the racial division in the South put on a black man. But Oscar told Granz he had signed up for the whole tour.

Granz and JATP's musicians traveled on a leased bus from city to city. In most parts of the country, they ate their meals at upscale restaurants. And in cities where they played concerts, they stayed at the finest hotels, pairing up two to a room. Oscar's roommate on his first tour was the tenor saxophonist Flip Phillips, who was white. Oscar was having fun — playing cards with the guys, sharing meals and laughs, listening to stories of life on the road from Flip and the other veteran musicians.

But the fun leaked out of the adventure soon after the bus crossed into the southern states. None of the restaurants served black customers. When the JATP people needed a meal, Granz and the white musicians brought food from the restaurants out to their black colleagues on the bus.

In the cities, hotels refused rooms to blacks. The white musicians continued to stay in the finest hotels in the prosperous sections of town, while the black musicians had to settle for rundown rooms in the shabby neighborhoods where black citizens lived. Phillips apologized to Oscar when they split up each night, telling Oscar how ashamed he felt.

What Oscar felt was worse than shame. His spirits dropped away, and sometimes, on his first tours through the segregated South, despair overcame him. In his seedy hotel room in one southern city, Oscar sniffed the stale smell of ancient cigar smoke in the air, examined the thin towel over the dirty sink in the corner and the even thinner blanket on the sagging bed, and shuddered at the sight of the pail of sand in the corner that he was supposed to use as a urinal.

How had he come to such a low and miserable state? He was an artist, a well-known piano player. People paid money to listen to him. And yet he was looked on as a man who deserved only second-class treatment, all because of the color of his skin.

Oscar lay on the terrible bed in the terrible room and wept.

———

Norman Granz struggled to win rights for JATP's black musicians, carrying on the fight he had begun in the California clubs. The victories came slowly. In concert halls in the South, black patrons were limited to seats in the balconies. Granz used JATP's financial leverage – they always sold out their concerts – to pressure some halls into desegregating the seating. So determined was Granz that, arguing his black musicians' cause in a hall in Houston, Texas, he stood up to a white police detective who held a gun on him. The armed cop backed away.

Still, it took years before Granz persuaded the top hotels that his black musicians had the same right to stay there as his white musicians. Restaurants continued to refuse black customers for at least another decade and a half. It was all part of the everyday humiliation of segregation that disheartened Oscar. Separate water fountains for blacks, separate public washrooms, separate entrances to buildings – he was always on his guard, afraid he'd take a wrong step. During JATP's southern tours, he thought his nerves were going to snap.

Oscar's anger and frustration over the racial insults he so often faced didn't show up in his music. He played with force, not with rage. Perhaps, no matter how much racism cost him in heartache, Oscar was too much the reticent and polite Canadian to permit his music to reflect his feelings.

Unlike Oscar, several black American jazz musicians made statements about racial injustice in their music. The playing of the brilliant and combative bassist and composer Charles Mingus radiated anger. One of his best-known compositions, "Fables of Faubus," represented an attack on Orval Faubus, the governor of Arkansas, who was cruel and unscrupulous in opposing school desegregation in his state.

The Mingus approach wasn't for Oscar. He composed a song about race and civil rights, but it offered hope and not a hint of anger. Oscar wrote the piece in the course of a trio recording session produced by Norman Granz in 1962. When the trio had taped several tunes, Granz asked for one more, something with a deep blues feel to it.

For inspiration, Oscar drew on the black spirituals he knew as a kid in St. Henri. He came up with a simple, righteous melodic line, and as he played it, the other members of his trio picked up the melody and the gently rocking rhythm.

Granz loved the tune, and when he asked Oscar for a title for this new and deeply felt number, Oscar's mind turned to Martin Luther King Jr. and the civil rights movement. "Call it 'Hymn to Freedom,'" Oscar said.

A few months later, Granz hired a woman named Harriette Hamilton to write lyrics for the song. Hamilton worked with a famous black American choir called the Malcolm Dodds Singers. Her lyrics began, "When every heart joins every heart and together yearns for liberty, That's when we'll be free. . . ."

"Hymn to Freedom" was Oscar's first significant composition and probably his most popular. It was recorded more often by other musicians, both with and without Harriette Hamilton's lyrics, than anything else he wrote. As an anthem, it had a mellow, uplifting feel — a combination that made it appropriate for just about any solemn public occasion. Choirs performed "Hymn to Freedom" as a tribute to Queen Elizabeth during her Golden Jubilee visit to Canada in 2003 and at Barack Obama's presidential inauguration celebration in Washington, DC, in 2008.

As a young musician, Oscar conducted himself in all situations as a responsible citizen. Norman Granz recognized his qualities when he made Oscar JATP's straw boss on concert nights. The informal title meant that Oscar was the musician who took over many of Granz's duties. Though Oscar was as much as two or three decades younger than some of the other musicians, he was the one Granz assigned to get everybody onstage, on time, in tune, and ready to play. Oscar often counted off the tempos and reminded soloists of their allotted number of solo choruses.

Oscar was dependable in everything. In personal habits, he drank moderately. He smoked, but he regularly took up cures to kick the habit. The trouble was, every time he swore off smoking cigarettes and puffing on his beautiful pipes, his weight shot up. If Oscar committed any of the seven deadly sins, it was gluttony. He loved to eat – he loved to cook, too – and he remained a very large man throughout his entire life.

Drugs presented a dilemma for Oscar. Soft drugs – marijuana, hashish – were common in the jazz community. Louis Armstrong smoked a marijuana joint every night of his working life to relax him during the grind of one-nighters he played into his early seventies. Oscar developed no such habit, but he didn't make a fuss about other jazz musicians' comfort with the drug.

Hard drugs – heroin, cocaine – were another matter. Early in Oscar's touring career, he was invited to a party in Baltimore for the great singer Billie Holiday. When Oscar arrived, he realized that the guests, including Billie, were stoned on something. What kind of drug were these people into? Pretty soon, a bottle of white powder was passed Oscar's way. He looked closer at the bottle and felt a chill go through him. The white powder was cocaine. Oscar left Billie Holiday's party in a rush.

"I knew for certain I didn't belong at that party," Oscar later wrote. Both his upbringing in Montreal and his common sense told him that cocaine was not good for his health and definitely bad for his music. He didn't see how a man could make jazz when he didn't have firm control on his instrument and his imagination.

If cocaine was bad, as far as Oscar was concerned the highly addictive heroin was worse. In the bebop years, heroin raced through jazz like a scourge. Most people pinned the blame on Charlie Parker. Hooked on heroin for much of his short life, Parker was still one of jazz's creative geniuses. Nobody in modern jazz could match his level of improvisation, and impressionable young musicians got the misguided idea that heroin went with genius. If they wanted to play like Parker, they needed to shoot drugs like him. Heroin led many of them not to creativity but to prison, ill health, an early death, or a combination of all three.

Oscar looked on drug addicts with pity and scorn, an attitude that was reinforced on the night of his Carnegie Hall debut. After the concert, Oscar dropped into Birdland, New York's leading jazz club for many years, where a tenor saxophonist Oscar admired was scheduled to play. But as Oscar made his way through the club, he spotted the tenor man slumped across a booth, collapsed in a drug-induced stupor.

Oscar felt sickened. Someone had draped around the saxophonist's neck a hotel room sign reading DO NOT DISTURB.

Ironically, Oscar frequently played in JATP concerts and recording sessions with Charlie Parker. Parker was so celebrated as a musician that Birdland was named after him – "Bird" was Parker's nickname. While Oscar acknowledged Parker's enormous artistry, he didn't think much of Parker's morality or the example he set for the jazz musicians who followed him.

If Oscar was asked for his advice to young musicians about the perils of injecting heroin, he'd reply, "I'd say your instrument should be your needle and music your addiction. It is mine."

Straight-arrow that Oscar was, he never took an activist approach to the moral and racial issues that affected jazz. He didn't preach about drugs, and he wasn't noisy in his opposition to racism. He had little or no part in freedom marches and demonstrations. That kind of public confrontational approach wasn't Oscar's style.

Still, watching Canadian television in 1980, he became aware of something he considered racist, and the sight filled him with disgust. What Oscar couldn't help noticing on TV was that nobody in the commercials looked like him. In every advertisement, no matter what product it promoted, all of the people were white.

Oscar resented the exclusion of blacks. Did beer advertisers and the agencies that made their commercials think black people didn't drink Molson's beer? Did advertising people suppose blacks never brushed their teeth with Colgate or ate Rice Krispies for breakfast?

By ignoring black consumers, Oscar realized that the TV advertisers were practicing a subtle but dispiriting form of racism.

As Oscar was wondering what, if anything, he could do about this type of discrimination, a Canadian journalist named Gene Lees was writing a profile of Oscar for *Toronto Life* magazine. Oscar and Lees went back a long way together. Years earlier in Hamilton, when the barber refused to cut Oscar's hair, Lees was the junior reporter at the *Spectator* who wrote some of the newspaper's stories about the barbershop episode.

Lees was a knowledgeable jazz fan, and his later career took him into full-time jazz journalism. Moving to the United States, he edited *DownBeat* magazine for several years, then wrote countless books and magazine articles about jazz. In the process, he became a particular friend to Oscar and a champion of his music.

In the *Toronto Life* profile, Lees and Oscar decided to give big play to Oscar's criticism of Canadian television's racist commercials. Their decision had major consequences when Roy McMurtry read the article. McMurtry was Ontario's attorney general, a politician who emphasized human rights in his portfolio. He thought Oscar's ideas about racism on TV fit into the overall McMurtry approach to rights issues.

Roy McMurtry, Ontario's attorney general from 1975 to 1985, worked with Oscar in a successful campaign against "unconscious" racism in Canada's advertising industry.

An affable, low-key operator, McMurtry believed in nego-tiation behind the scenes as a useful tool in attacking problems. True to his style, McMurtry arranged a series of lunch meetings at the exclusive Albany Club in Toronto. He invited advertising executives and marketing people to talk about racism in com-mercials. At most meetings, McMurtry brought Oscar along as his guest. Over lunch, McMurtry sat back while Oscar expanded on the points he made in the *Toronto Life* article.

During his years of addressing jazz fans in concert halls and nightclubs, Oscar had developed into an assured and effective public speaker. At the McMurtry lunches, he turned on all his persuasive charm. He thought he was having a positive impact, which turned out to be largely the case. Though there remained doubters among the advertising executives, the majority decided that eloquent Oscar had scored winning points. They promised to see what they could do about the commercials.

Changes didn't come overnight, but in time, new rounds of commercials began to reflect the audience that was watching them. In order to appeal to a wide spectrum of viewers, the advertisers cast actors of every color. Soon enough, when Oscar turned on his TV set, he could now see people like himself eating cereal, drinking beer, and carrying on like other ordinary Canadians.

Oscar conceded that what he accomplished was hardly a dramatic blow against racism. Desegregating TV commercials in Canada wasn't in the same league as the deadly confrontations that had earlier brought new freedoms to blacks in the American South. But Oscar felt vindicated that the straight-arrow approach he championed all his life had won a small part of the struggle for black rights in Canadian society.

CHAPTER EIGHT

OSCAR'S TRIO FINDS ITS GROOVE

n an early August evening in 1956, Oscar was telling everybody that he felt more relaxed with his music than he ever had in his life.

For part of that August week, the Oscar Peterson Trio was performing in the southwestern Ontario town of Stratford. Stratford had attracted recent attention as the home of a summer drama festival devoted to Shakespeare's plays. In 1956, the festival was in its fourth year and on its way to great renown. Each summer, the festival ran a parallel program of music concerts, and that year, the Oscar Peterson Trio was invited to play. It was sharing the bill for two midweek August nights with the cerebral New York group the Modern Jazz Quartet. (Over the years, Oscar's groups had simple names; depending on size, they were called the Oscar Peterson Trio, the Oscar Peterson Quartet, and, rarely, the Oscar Peterson Quintet.)

In the relaxed Oscar's view, the appearance at Stratford came at a time when his trio had moved into a long period of unprecedented performances. All three musicians in the group – Oscar, Ray Brown, the guitarist Herb Ellis – were on fire with drive and imagination.

Oscar had put the trio together in 1953, with the instrumentation inspired by the 1940s trio of his hero, Nat Cole. And now Oscar thought his own trio's music was as good as it got in jazz. He felt so positive that he persuaded Norman Granz to record the Stratford performance and release it as a concert LP.

The subsequent record album – titled *The Oscar Peterson Trio at the Stratford Shakespearean Festival* – grasped a historic moment. All three musicians in the trio agreed that, far more than any studio recording, the Stratford album presented them the way they played every single night during their triumphant run through the 1950s.

"We reached musical and emotional heights you don't reach very often," Herb Ellis said of the group.

Jazz critics and the jazz public agreed with Ellis. When the Stratford album was released, reviewers were virtually unanimous in writing glowing notices. And of Oscar's many dozens of albums, it ranked near the top in sales, was reissued frequently, and remained available for decades.

Backstage, before a concert at Toronto's Massey Hall in February 1965, Oscar took time to explain a musical point for the author, Jack Batten. The trumpet hanging on the coat hook behind Oscar belonged to the great Roy Eldridge.

The date of the recording was August 9, the second night of the trio's Stratford booking. If Oscar felt relaxed – and he kept saying so – he owed part of his ease to having John Lewis in the recording booth. Lewis was the pianist and music director for the Modern Jazz Quartet (made up of piano, vibraphone, bass, and drums). Since the MJQ and Oscar's trio shared several dual bookings like the one in Stratford, Lewis grew familiar with the trio's work. He offered to sit in the booth with Granz after the MJQ played the first half of the concert. He would help ensure that the recording caught the Peterson group's sound and balance.

Oscar must have thanked his lucky stars that Lewis had volunteered. Although Oscar had nothing but the warmest feelings for his regular producer and dear friend Norman Granz, Granz was known to turn out more than a few sloppy records. Since he often seemed to care mostly about getting records completed on time and on budget, jazz's nuances could slip by Granz without him noticing.

Nuance was John Lewis's middle name. The pieces he wrote for the MJQ were built on delicacy and subtlety. Though this understated approach put Lewis in a different jazz camp than Oscar, he understood what the Peterson trio was all about. He appreciated Oscar's power and rollicking swing, and he had sound ideas about capturing the group's essence in the Stratford recording.

The trio played eleven numbers that night. Each ran between four and nine minutes, with one exceptional track stretching to thirteen minutes. The tunes included one by Duke Ellington, two of Oscar's own compositions, and one written by the somewhat eccentric pianist and composer Thelonious Monk. For the rest of the material, Oscar dipped into movies and Broadway musicals, playing what he considered the best from both sources (as in all concerts, music licensing agencies collected royalties on the songs that were performed, passing on the fees to each song's composer or license holder).

One of these tunes was a Broadway number called "How High the Moon." Beboppers had seized on the song so often and with such enthusiasm over the years that fans thought of it as the official bop anthem.

At Stratford, the audience clapped in recognition of the first familiar notes of Oscar's version of "How High the Moon." Here was a tune everybody knew. Little did the listeners realize that Oscar was in the process of messing up their expectations. While the beboppers usually played the song up-tempo, with all guns blazing, Oscar and his trio slowed the pace to a surprising lope.

In his solo, Oscar sailed ahead with long, tuneful single-note passages. Then, staying comfortable with the laid-back beat, he eased into a finale of swirling, two-handed chords. It was a typical performance by Oscar in his no-pressure, no-sweat mode.

By contrast, the treatment of Duke Ellington's good-natured "Love You Madly" dripped in sweat before Oscar was finished. Overall, the number showcased Oscar's talent for creating a thrilling atmosphere, then doubling up on the thrills.

At about the two-thirds mark in the song, after several quietly passionate passages at a medium tempo, Oscar went into a series of extra-large, two-handed chord rolls, the kind that threw listeners, metaphorically, against the back of their seats. Pulling off this dramatic switch in sound and tempo called for all of Oscar's self-assurance and technique.

On both "How High the Moon" and "Love You Madly," there seemed to be a fourth instrument joining the trio that sounded like a primitive drum. It was actually Oscar's foot. When he played, he had a habit of tapping his right shoe, which was large and heavy. The microphones, as well as the listeners' ears, couldn't help but pick up the thumping shoe.

Oscar made vocal sounds, too, some of them discernible on many Stratford tracks. The sounds were between a hum and a growl, in company with his improvisations. Both the mumbles and the foot-tapping were regarded fondly by most of Oscar's devoted fans. The sounds weren't distractions to these listeners but idiosyncrasies that had their place in the Peterson musical package.

As the Stratford concert moved along, Oscar and the trio gave a neat and tidy treatment to "52nd Street Theme," a tune written by Thelonious Monk. At the piano, Monk made an odd figure. He held his fingers flat over the keyboard and seemed to stagger into the keys. Oscar regarded Monk's lack of technique as an offense to jazz pianists everywhere. It baffled him that critics and many fans looked on Monk as a towering jazz figure.

As a composer, Monk wrote dozens of songs that remain in the standard jazz repertoire today. The tunes are often difficult, full of jagged melodic lines and strange dissonant chords. Oscar's personal playlist concentrated on Monk's early and more conservative work. He sometimes played "Round Midnight," a lovely ballad, which was the best known of Monk's songs.

And with the trio of the 1950s, Oscar liked to work over "52nd Street Theme," a Monk number in a boppish vein. Oscar's version was quick and certain, rounding off the jagged lines. At this point in his career – Oscar was now thirty – he had developed unshakeable confidence in his own musical judgment. More than once, he made it clear in interviews that when he sat at the piano, he was playing only as himself. He made every song his personal property – not the composer's, not anybody's except his own – even songs by a generally revered composer like Monk.

The 1950s Oscar Peterson Trio of Oscar, bassist Ray Brown, and guitarist Herb Ellis identified the Peterson brand as jazz with plenty of imagination and power.

Oscar worked out arrangements for practically all of his trio's songs. Other jazz trios operated more simply. On each number, they played the melody, the pianist soloed, the other musicians took brief solos, then everyone returned to the melody for the final chorus that rode the song out. But with Oscar's trio, the tunes had much more varied structures, more intricate interplay among the three instruments, and lots of room for Brown and Ellis to show their stuff in both ensemble and solo.

On only "Falling in Love with Love," a waltz from a Broadway show, did Oscar stick to a more regular structure, one that allowed lots of solo space for himself and shorter solos for the others. Bracketing the solos were Oscar and Herb Ellis playing the melody in gorgeous unison.

Ellis, a pale red-haired Texan, was four years older than Oscar. Like all guitarists his age, he owed his style to a largely unschooled kid from Oklahoma City named Charlie Christian. Until Christian came along in the late 1930s, the guitar in jazz was strictly a rhythm instrument. In jazz bands of all sizes, it was confined to the job of joining with the bass and drums in keeping the beat on the move. Guitarists were virtually never permitted solo space.

Then Christian emerged on the scene, playing single-note solos in the style of a jazz horn. Christian's particular horn influence was the cool and concise tenor saxophonist Lester Young. It almost seemed that Christian was translating Young from tenor to guitar as he ripped off long shimmering lines of improvisation. Christian's playing captivated everyone who heard it. In 1939, Benny Goodman scooped him up for his band, where Christian was given a chance to showcase his sensational guitar solos to a wide audience.

As a pioneer, Christian had a short time to enjoy fame. Tuberculosis led to his death in March 1942, when he was just twenty-five years old. But Christian's impact on other guitarists was immediate and lasting. Herb Ellis described his first hearing of Christian on the Goodman records as the equivalent of "a spiritual awakening."

Ellis wasted no time in recasting himself as a Christian-style player. After paying his jazz dues in Jimmy Dorsey's well-known big band and in a sophisticated trio called the Soft Winds, Ellis was hired by Oscar in 1953 to fill out his trio. Ellis was exactly the guitarist to handle the group's tricky ensemble passages and to challenge Oscar with his inventive solos.

When the Oscar Peterson Trio took to the road for long stretches – booked by Norman Granz virtually nonstop in jazz clubs and concert halls in every major American and European city – Ellis and Ray Brown roomed together. They developed rituals. Every morning, they played golf together. Every afternoon, they rehearsed together. Every night, they went to work ready to deluge Oscar with the ideas about rhythms and harmonies they had developed that afternoon.

Oscar set the highest imaginable standards for himself and for the other two trio members. That was okay with Brown and Ellis. They wanted to excel as much as Oscar did. Why else were the two rehearsing every day?

During the 1956 Stratford concert, Oscar, Ellis, and Brown showed the rewards of all the hard work they'd put into their music. The uncanny control they had over their instruments at the highest velocity was on particular display at the concert with their version of a song called "Swinging on a Star." The number originated in a 1944 movie titled *Going My Way* starring Bing Crosby, who sang "Swinging on a Star" in the film. *Going My Way* won three Oscars that year: one for Best Picture, a second for Crosby as Best Actor, and a third for "Swinging on a Star" as Best Original Song. The

Crosby version was warm, lilting, and humorous – nothing like the interpretation that the Oscar Peterson Trio came up with at Stratford.

The trio took the tune at a pace opposite to a lilt. It was more like a charge in which the three musicians maintained a scalding tempo in both ensemble and solos. Speed can be a jazz musician's downfall, leading to flubbed technique and musical goofs. But that wasn't close to a problem with Oscar, Ellis, and Brown. Each player was steady as a rock. And no matter how breakneck the speed, each appeared never to miss a note, soloing with as much invention as anybody could produce at such an unyielding rhythm.

The trio slowed things down, but just by a beat or two, on the tune that followed, "Noreen's Nocturne." Oscar wrote it as a tip of his hat to Noreen Nimmons, the wife of Toronto clarinetist, composer, and Peterson pal Phil Nimmons. In music, "nocturne" refers to a dreamy piece. Oscar's notion of nocturne in the one he composed for Noreen was more eyes wide-open than dreamy. While the melody had a contemplative quality, the trio was more interested in having a boisterous good time. They succeeded, riding the song at a gallop for its entire length.

"Flamingo" offered the audience a chance to catch its breath. The song had the slower feel of a ballad and was best known to jazz fans in a 1941 version recorded by Duke Ellington with his singer, Herb Jeffries. Jeffries sang in a lush baritone voice, and he gave "Flamingo" a highly melodramatic interpretation. Oscar and his trio took the same approach, and Oscar assumed the role of Jeffries, playing with impossibly grand flourishes and lots of high-flown chords. The song packed in so much melodrama that the Stratford listeners might have assumed Oscar was kidding a little. He probably was, abandoning the serious stuff for one number and having some lighthearted fun.

When Ed Thigpen's drums replaced Herb Ellis's guitar in the trio with Oscar and Ray Brown in the 1960s, the music remained polished and took on a new force.

Humor was a quality that Oscar and the other musicians often brought to the job in clubs and concerts. Oscar and Ray especially loved to play practical jokes on one another, anything to relieve the stress of long days on the road. It was mostly kid stuff – pranks that made the other guy look silly or embarrassed. Childish or not, Oscar and Brown were known in the jazz community as world-class jokesters.

Oscar liked fooling around with Brown's bass during concert intermissions, loosening the G-string and tuning it way down. Then he distracted Brown before they started the concert's second half, giving Brown no chance to find and fix the detuning before the trio resumed playing. In the first number, when Ray hit the G-string, he got nothing except homely twangs and thumps. Oscar always laughed himself silly at Brown's predicament.

Brown's favorite revenge involved the little steel balls from a game called Pachinko. Ray secretly scattered the little balls across the strings of Oscar's piano at intermission. When Oscar started playing, the miniature balls bounced on the strings, making loud and dissonant pings that everybody found comic – everyone except Oscar.

One joke that Ray thought up as a way to rattle Oscar centered on the great pianist Art Tatum. Fans and critics in the 1950s had already begun describing Oscar's technique and drive as equal to the great Tatum's. Flattered as Oscar was, he felt comparisons were premature.

Nevertheless he remained in awe of Tatum, whom he had not yet met. He got the shakes every time he even thought about the day when the two might run across one another. Brown took advantage of Oscar's dread of finding himself in the same room with Tatum.

"Hey," Brown would say, when the trio was playing in a nightclub, "I think I see Tatum at a table over there!"

"Oh, no!" Oscar always reacted with horror, his fingers going limp on the keyboard. "I'm not ready for this!"

After a few adrenalin-draining moments, Oscar would realize that Tatum wasn't in the room. Tatum was never in the room, and after a while, Oscar stopped reacting to Brown's supposed Tatum sightings.

Then came the night in 1954 when the trio was working a Washington, DC, jazz club.

"I don't believe this," Brown said to Oscar between numbers. "Art Tatum's over there at the bar."

"Come on, man," Oscar answered. "You've pulled that trick too many times."

"But tonight I'm not fooling," Ray insisted.

"Well, I'm not falling for it again."

A little later, as the trio played, Oscar glanced in the direction of the bar. He looked, and did a double take. Tatum was really sitting at the bar.

"Oh my god!" Oscar said. His hands froze. He could barely pull himself together to finish the tune.

During intermission, Ray Brown dragged Oscar to the bar for an introduction. Oscar later described himself as "totally fright-ened" to meet Tatum. But Tatum turned out to be friendly and welcoming. He invited Oscar to join him at an after-hours club later that night. Oscar accepted.

At the club, Tatum asked Oscar to play. As soon as Oscar got a grip on himself, he zipped through several adroit choruses of "Tea for Two." Oscar had made an audacious choice. As he was aware, Tatum played "Tea for Two" so often that he practically owned the rights to it.

After Oscar finished, Tatum told him, "As long as I'm alive, I don't figure I'm going to let you have it," he said, referring to the song. "But you're the next after me."

Later on, thinking about Art Tatum's words, Oscar decided Tatum might have been using "Tea for Two" as a metaphor. What Tatum really meant was that he saw Oscar as his eventual successor. Oscar would be the jazz pianist who ruled all other jazz pianists after Tatum was gone. Tatum had said so in exactly those words.

Tatum and Peterson became close friends, but there were only a couple of years left for the friendship to mature. In early November 1956, Tatum fell seriously ill in Los Angeles. Oscar, who was working in San Francisco, said he would hurry down to visit Tatum as soon as his job allowed. But he didn't get to Los Angeles in time. Tatum died of kidney failure at age forty-seven.

At the Stratford Festival concert, Oscar's Tatumesque side was obvious in many tunes. "Gypsy in My Soul" offered one outstanding example. The song came from an unlikely source, having been written by two University of Pennsylvania students for a college occasion. The song gradually attained wider popularity and assumed a place on the playlist of many jazz musicians.

Oscar's treatment was taken at a medium tempo. It allowed much solo space for Ray Brown, who acquitted himself wonderfully in the song's Stratford performance. But more than just Brown, "Gypsy in My Soul" was notable for the energy that all three musicians put into their playing. Oscar contributed solos with Tatum-like runs and asides. The song hummed and throbbed in a show of technique that was just about impeccable.

"Nuages" demonstrated the same qualities. The song had been written in the 1930s by the French gypsy guitarist Django Reinhardt. Reinhardt came from a generation just before Oscar, and since the Frenchman rarely visited the United States, he acquired legendary status among jazz musicians on the basis of a handful of his records. He died in 1953, leaving behind the records and a few of his compositions. His best-known song, "Nuages," which means "clouds" in English, was a jazz favorite.

For the Peterson trio, the song was, fittingly, a guitar showcase for Herb Ellis. "Nuages" had a somewhat tricky melodic line. Ellis negotiated the tricks with a deft touch, never falling into the traps that might fool lesser guitarists. The number was also fascinating for the way the whole trio picked up the shift into ensemble-playing at the end of Ellis's solo. This changing of gears was obvious to different degrees in every track on the album, reflected in the way the three musicians fell into its all-hands-together swing mode as each one wound up a solo. But on "Nuages," the transition seemed especially adroit and authentic.

"How About You" found the trio in a playful frame of mind. The song came from a 1941 movie titled *Babes on Broadway*, starring Judy Garland and Mickey Rooney. "How About You" had lyrics that kidded around with language and images. The melody matched the attitudes of the words, and the Peterson trio picked up on the song's all-round good cheer. The musicians tossed the melody back and forth, rather like a juggling act in which nobody drops the ball. While Ellis stole the solo limelight, the song was another example of the trio's fundamental unity.

———

In early 1955, a couple of years after Oscar put together his Brown and Ellis trio, a period of strain hit the group. Oscar was on one side, Brown and Ellis on the other. The two rhythm players, Brown especially, thought Oscar didn't show proper appreciation for the level of their music or for the work they put in to reach that level. Oscar never patted the other two guys on the back, never congratulated them, and rarely flashed a smile. Mostly — rather like Oscar's father, back in the days when the Peterson kids were trying to master their lessons — Oscar just looked dissatisfied.

Brown finally blew up on a night when, in his opinion, Oscar was particularly unfair in ignoring Brown's and Ellis's contributions. It happened after a set in Chicago's premier jazz club, the London House. Brown thought he and Ellis had played brilliantly. But at the end of the evening, Oscar offered nothing except a grumpy expression.

"Just what do you expect from this group?" Brown demanded.

"Only a little music," Oscar answered dismissively.

Brown stomped off to get a drink, leaving Oscar wondering whether there was a problem he was unaware of.

A couple of hours later, alone in his hotel room, Oscar listened to a tape of the performance that night. He recognized that the music was pretty darn good. On some tunes, it was terrific. The version of "Sweet Georgia Brown" couldn't be topped.

He phoned Brown's room and woke him up. Oscar said, "'Sweet Georgia Brown' was just great!"

Brown barked, "We knew that last night!" Then he slammed down the receiver.

———

Just before Oscar stepped onstage at Massey Hall in Toronto in February 1965, he felt relaxed enough to tell a funny story that cracked up the author, Jack Batten.

In reaction to the phone-slamming, Oscar set out to diagnose his motives and attitudes. He decided that the reason behind the tension between him and the two other musicians was simple: He was paying too much attention to his own playing and not taking the time to catch what the other guys were up to.

"I was just so intent on doing my own particular thing," Oscar told Gene Lees. "I was not reacting to my group properly. At different times, we'd tape ourselves, and I'd hear these things go by, and I'd say, 'God *damn* it, they did *that*, they had *that* thing going, and I didn't take advantage of it!'"

Once Oscar figured out that his own failures were getting in the way, he made amends to Brown and Ellis. On a fresh note of compatibility, the trio winged off in a run that carried them to their ranking as one of the most acclaimed of all jazz trios.

Through these years and beyond, Oscar continued to be a

consistent winner of the *DownBeat* readers' poll as Best Jazz Pianist. Brown won almost as many polls as Best Jazz Bassist. The victories were only the beginning for Oscar. During his career, he won eight Grammy Awards for Best Jazz Performance, a string that culminated in his 1997 Grammy for Instrumental Soloist Lifetime Achievement Award.

As far as Canadians were concerned, Oscar was more than just an outstanding musician. In his native country, Oscar won status as a distinguished citizen. He was named an Officer of the Order of Canada in 1972 and was promoted to the Companion of the Order of Canada twelve years later. Twelve Canadian universities granted him honorary degrees, and between 1991 and 1994, he served as Chancellor of York University in Toronto. In 1993, Prime Minister Jean Chrétien planned to name Oscar Ontario's lieutenant governor, but Oscar suffered an illness that year, ruling out the appointment.

Such grand recognition began for Oscar with the trio of Brown, Ellis and himself, the group that established Oscar's musical approaches and ideas, forming the lifetime basis for the music he made as a dominant jazz pianist.

For the final number at the 1956 Stratford Festival concert, Oscar presented a thirteen-minute suite he had written called "Daisy's Dream." The Daisy of the title probably referred to his sister, though later he renamed the piece "The Music Box Suite."

According to Oscar, in writing the suite, he was inspired by John Lewis, the man in the recording booth that night. For his own group, the Modern Jazz Quartet, Lewis wrote several long pieces that featured fugues and rondos. He introduced themes, then repeated them in both written and improvised variations. Oscar included this aspect of Lewis's music in his own "Daisy's Dream."

The piece opened with a touching little melody. The trio played the passage with measured dignity, slow and slightly grand. It featured Ray Brown's bass, bowed not plucked. Then, just as the section threatened to overplay the grandeur, the suite slipped into a waltz.

The three instruments mixed themes in lively counterpoint until Oscar's piano took charge. Under his hand, the suite went all out for jazz. It was the trio at its most familiar. "Daisy's Dream" may have set the scene with a touching melody and a perfect waltz, but when the three musicians felt most comfortable, they played jazz that went in a spirit of "damn the torpedoes, full speed ahead." That was how they played on this section of the suite. Oscar's own solo ran to hundreds of notes per chorus, his right foot pounded the floor, and the trio charged.

At the eleven-minute mark of "Daisy's Dream," the musicians pulled back and returned to the opening theme. Over the final bars, the music remained sweet and gentle, and on this subdued note the suite concluded. But as the audience broke into a sustained ovation, it was a good bet that it wasn't the passage at the end they were cheering. Neither was it the fugues and rondos and the bits of semiclassical music. What got the audience on its feet and celebrating were the lengthy and powerful jazz passages.

This was the real Oscar Peterson — the kind of extroverted music that made him the long-reigning king of jazz piano.

CHAPTER NINE

GRIEF, TROUBLE, AND CHANGE

I n November 1956, Oscar's father, Daniel, suffered a massive stroke. At the time, Oscar and his trio were playing a nightclub date in San Francisco. It was the same month when Art Tatum fell ill. Oscar promised to visit Tatum on his sickbed, but before he could keep the promise, word reached Oscar of his father's stroke, and he rushed home to Montreal.

Daniel's doctors offered little hope of his recovery. The stroke had been too powerful, and as the doctors had warned, Daniel soon died. Art Tatum passed away that same week. In the space of a few days, Oscar lost his father and his idol among jazz pianists.

Two years earlier, when Oscar and the trio were playing a week at the Town Tavern, the popular Toronto jazz club on Queen Street, he invited his father from Montreal to listen to the music. At the Town, when word got around that Oscar's father was in the house – Oscar often introduced him from the bandstand – people flocked to Daniel's table. They congratulated him on being the father of such an accomplished musician. They praised Oscar, and by extension, they were praising Daniel. It turned into one of the proudest weeks of Daniel's life.

When his father died, Oscar's great regret was that he hadn't given Daniel more treats like the week in Toronto. He wished he had taken Daniel on the road with him. He wished his father had lived long enough to see Oscar's career climb higher, to see Oscar take off as a star of the jazz world. Oscar realized how much Daniel had sacrificed for him and his siblings. Whatever personal dreams Daniel may have had as a musician, he had never been in a position to realize them. Oscar was pretty sure his father had at least fulfilled those dreams vicariously through Oscar's magnificent success.

Much later, when Oscar was as old as his father was when he died, he said it dawned on him at last that Daniel's tough discipline as a music teacher was exactly what Oscar and the other kids needed at their young ages. Oscar's future as a pianist depended on those early lessons of practice and hard work. He appreciated Daniel's importance to his career and wrote that Daniel was in all ways "an outstanding man."

————

For one of Oscar's record albums produced by Norman Granz (left), Oscar accompanied the great singer and dancer Fred Astaire (middle). Astaire not only sang in his intimate and joyful style on the album, he also added some highly rhythmic tap dances to the recording.

Oscar's mother, Olivia, now a widow, carried the double health burden of diabetes and severe arthritis. She couldn't manage life on her own, and May, the youngest of the Peterson children, moved in, serving as her mother's nurse, helper, and loving caregiver. The arrangement gave Olivia a reasonably decent life for the following fourteen years, until she died in 1970 of complications from her diabetes.

After Olivia's death, Oscar recognized he had shortchanged his mother in the credit she deserved in advancing his career. Daniel may have been the parent with the musical knowledge, but Olivia's quiet encouragement had been just as essential. She knew all the right buttons to push with Oscar. When he was still a teenager, he complained about his lack of a recording contract. Olivia offered a simple suggestion: "Phone the people who make the records," she said. A small lightbulb went on over Oscar's head. He made the call to Hugh Joseph, and his life as an RCA Victor recording artist began.

In the early 1960s, Phil Nimmons, the Canadian clarinetist and composer, joined Oscar in organizing their own Toronto school for teaching young musicians the art of playing jazz.

Olivia made other contributions to Oscar's musical and social development. As the deeply religious member of the Peterson household, Olivia insisted on church services and Sunday school at Union United for all the kids. She urged them to make use of the Negro Community Center, borrowing the brass instruments and taking the free lessons that taught them how to play the trumpet and cornet and trombone. And she lined the kids up for roles in the band that played at Sunday afternoon meetings of the Universal Negro Improvement Association.

"It is only now," Oscar wrote long after Olivia's death, "that I truly realize how much of her life she gave up in trying to be a good mother."

By the early 1960s, Oscar's marriage to Lil was broken beyond repair. Lil wasn't made for the role of wife to an itinerant jazz musician – she longed for a conventional family life with a conventional husband. Oscar, the extraordinary jazzman, was the last thing from conventional.

Separation and divorce soon followed. Oscar moved out of the family home into the first of a series of Toronto apartments he rented. Lil continued to raise the five kids, supported by Oscar's payments of alimony and child support. Oscar and Lil remained on friendly terms until Lil, who never remarried, died of a sudden heart attack in 1983.

After the separation, Oscar saw as much of his five kids as such a busy traveling man could manage. And he made sure they all took music lessons. While none of them chose careers in music, they'd learned enough to appreciate their father's remarkable

Oscar was looking for inspiration in instructing a young pianist at his Toronto jazz school. He sent many graduates into success in the jazz world.

contribution to jazz. Oscar Junior came closest to the jazz life, often contributing as an engineer at his father's recording sessions. The three girls – Lynn, Sharon, and Gay – all married and concentrated on raising their families. Norman, the youngest, chose horticulture as his field, starting out in the parks department of North York.

One spot where Oscar liked to gather with his children was the property he bought in Haliburton cottage country, 132 miles

(214 kilometers) north of Toronto. Oscar's cottage was on a lake in Harcourt Park, a vast area of woods and lakes not far from the mighty Algonquin Park. It was a refuge for Oscar, the one place where he was completely at peace, where he could enjoy nature and the company of his children.

One autumn day, Oscar Junior was staying with his father at the cottage. The two Oscars were raking leaves on the front lawn when a car stopped on the local road. The man at the wheel told them he was looking for a gardener to tend his property and asked if Oscar Senior was interested.

"Sure," Oscar answered deadpan. "As soon as we finish my place."

"What?" the man said. "You live here?" Then be blushed, realizing he'd made a terrible blunder.

The car sped away, and when Oscar told the story in later years, he was more amused than enraged at the man's racial profiling.

A more joyous Peterson cottage experience came one August 15th in the 1970s. Oscar was sitting on his dock, enjoying a drink with a couple of friends. After a while, he couldn't help noticing that an unusual number of boats were heading toward his place: rowboats, canoes, small motorboats, enough to add up to a flotilla. Oscar was puzzled, maybe a trifle alarmed.

Then the young people in the boats began to raise banners. HAPPY BIRTHDAY, OSCAR, the banners read. They broke into a chorus of "Happy Birthday." *Yes, of course, it's my birthday*, Oscar thought, *but how do these kids know?* Oscar never found out, but he was deeply moved by the kids' gesture. It was just another reason he loved his times at the cottage.

———

On an exceptionally cold February night in 1965, Oscar played a concert at Massey Hall in Toronto. Twenty minutes before the concert began, five excited kids joined the crowd of musicians and their friends in the greenroom backstage. The kids were Oscar's sons and daughters, shepherded by their mother, Lil. They bounced into the room, hugging people and offering smiles and kisses to everyone. One of the people they greeted was a tall, well-dressed woman. The Peterson kids and Lil knew her well. Her name was Sandy King, and she lived with Oscar. The kids knew her as Daddy's girlfriend.

Both Lil and Sandy were large, well-built women, but in every other way, Sandy was as different from Lil as day is from night. Sandy was white and came from an upper-middle-class Toronto background. Her father was vice president of personnel at the Simpsons-Sears department stores. For high school, Mr. King sent Sandy to the posh private school for girls, Havergal College. After graduation, Sandy studied nursing, and at the time she met Oscar, she was an operating-room nurse.

Oscar and Sandy came together in the most appropriate of places. Late one night, in the small lobby of the Town Tavern, Sandy was leaving just as Oscar was arriving with a group of friends who had been touring the city's jazz spots. On the spur of the moment, Oscar asked Sandy to stay for another set. Just as spontaneously, Sandy agreed. She sat with Oscar and his friends, and before the night was out, both discovered they had much in common.

Sandy's affection for jazz reached back long before her meeting with Oscar. She loved jazz and the jazz life, working jazz slang into her everyday conversation. She hit it off with the members of Oscar's trio and with all his other jazz musician friends. They recognized that Sandy had a firm knowledge of the music. She was, as the musicians said, hip.

Soon Sandy moved in with Oscar. She accompanied him to concerts and club dates across North America and Europe. She was a confident traveler who knew how to handle herself in foreign cities. She gave up nursing in favor of a life devoted to Oscar. She was happy. So was Oscar.

One day in the mid-1960s, Oscar received a message that Mr. King, Sandy's father, wanted to talk with him. Since the two men already knew one another, Oscar thought, *Oh-oh, Mr. King may have reservations about his daughter living with a black man.* But Mr. King had no issues with Oscar's color. Instead, he asked Oscar to please marry Sandy. It was embarrassing to him and his wife that their daughter was living with a man who wasn't her husband. Couldn't Oscar just put their minds at ease?

So, not long after the conversation, Oscar and Sandy got married. It was a match made in jazz heaven.

CHAPTER TEN

SACRIFICE AND SUCCESS

ne morning in the spring of 1958, Oscar woke

to discover that his trio was missing a player.

He had arrived in Europe a few days earlier to

rehearse for a JATP tour that would cover Belgium, Holland,

and the Scandinavian countries. Stockholm, Sweden, was a terrific

jazz city, and JATP always drew large and adoring crowds there.

Norman Granz was billing the trio as the top stars on the tour. But

Oscar was short a guitarist because Herb Ellis hadn't shown up.

Ellis suffered from binge alcoholism. When he was on the job playing guitar, he drank liquor only now and again. But between engagements, when he had a few days of spare time, he couldn't resist alcohol. He drank himself into helplessness, disappeared, and missed trio gigs.

Each time Ellis fell victim to his demons — it happened three or four times a year — Oscar was generous. He would forgive his friend, telling him to just get back to making great jazz. But after years of this approach, Oscar learned that the soft treatment was a mistake. An alcoholic needed a tough hand to help him turn away from the booze that was destroying his life.

When Ellis arrived a few days into the 1958 European tour, apologetic and full of remorse, Oscar took a stronger stance. He warned Ellis that he was letting down the trio and damaging his health. He told Ellis he needed to do something drastic about his alcohol problem.

Ellis's solution was to upend his career. He told Oscar he was leaving the trio after the European tour and a few scheduled concerts back in North America. The grind of a jazzman's touring life wasn't any help in getting a grip on his drinking. Ellis was going home to California with his wife, Patti. He stood a better chance of winning his struggle against booze in peaceful, stable surroundings.

Near the end of July that summer, Ellis played his last concert with the trio in Hamilton, Ontario. It was Oscar's first visit to the city since the haircut episode. "OSCAR RETURNS, WITHOUT A

The wary expression on Oscar's face in this 1991 portrait was understandable. He had already suffered through health problems. Alas, even more serious physical setbacks lay ahead.

GRUDGE," read the headline in the *Spectator*. The headline was inaccurate. Oscar may not have held the city responsible for his humiliation in the barbershop, but a racial insult was one thing he never forgave.

The trio played the concert. Then, with regret on the part of all three men, Oscar and Ray Brown moved on to the next job. They played as a duo, while Ellis flew to Los Angeles to find the straight and narrow path.

He joined Alcoholics Anonymous, the organization that guided alcoholics through a lifelong rehab program. With AA's help, Ellis stayed away from temptation. He and Patti had two kids, and Ellis earned very good money playing in the orchestras for TV shows, movies, and advertising jingles.

Several years later, when his kids were close to becoming adults, Ellis was fed up making music in the commercial world. "Junk," he called it. With relief, he returned to jazz, rejoining Oscar's group for several concerts, club dates, and recordings.

Oscar recognized that Ellis hadn't lost his remarkable touch with the guitar. When he made his first new album with Ellis, Oscar gave him a heartfelt welcome back. He called the album *Hello, Herbie*.

Back in 1958, Oscar doubted a guitarist existed who could fill Ellis's shoes. He decided to hire a drummer for the trio instead. With a drummer, the trio would have a significant increase in power and a better chance of cutting through the noise at the big outdoor jazz festivals. And with a drummer in place of a guitarist, Oscar would have far more solo space for himself.

That was when Oscar signed Ed Thigpen.

The son of a big band drummer, Thigpen had all the right credentials. He swung, and he was versatile. He had experience working with a wide range of pianists, from avant-garde players like Lennie Tristano to mainstream stylists like Billy Taylor. He backed popular singers, Peggy Lee and Johnny Mathis among them. His work behind the vocalists showed Oscar that Thigpen could play with restraint and a delicate touch. Oscar liked those qualities in a drummer because they were needed in playing ballads with pianists.

Starting out with Oscar, there were periods when Thigpen felt intimidated. "On our worst night," Oscar told him, "we've got to sound better than most people sound on their best night." *Whoa*, Thigpen thought, *this was going to need some work.*

Ray Brown took Thigpen under his wing. On afternoons on the road, the two set up their instruments in Brown's hotel room and practiced what they called "time." The term covered the rhythmic patterns they would play behind Oscar, the groove they'd generate for the piano. Thigpen loved the sessions with Brown. To him, "time" was what jazz was all about.

While Thigpen brushed up his accompanist skills, he also grew into a more than passable soloist. Not every jazz fan had the patience for drum solos, which could be noisy and incoherent. But Thigpen won the listeners to his side with a personal solo strategy. He said his method was a matter of "crests."

In each solo, he would build a small crest of sound. Then he backed off, built a larger crest, and backed off again — but not for long before he'd build an even larger crest until it grew into an enormous one. And then he'd get out of it quickly and return to the rest of the trio. The method was guaranteed to win an ovation.

———

Guitarist Herb Ellis and bassist Ray Brown, the veterans of Oscar's formidable trio of the 1950s, found happiness and great music each time they rejoined Oscar for concerts in the 1980s and 1990s.

The handoff from Herb Ellis to Ed Thigpen was seamless. For Oscar's fans, the only question became which Peterson group was the greater – the trio with Ellis or the one with Thigpen? The contest was pretty much a draw.

If Thigpen won an edge, it was because of the 1962 album titled *Night Train*. As Ellis had before him, Thigpen recorded dozens of albums in his six years with the trio. Everything about Thigpen's period alongside Peterson and Brown echoed Ellis's. They worked the same grueling schedule of recording sessions and club dates; the same concerts in North America, Europe, and the Far East; the same number of TV shows and festivals. Everything was the same except that Thigpen had *Night Train* on his side.

On December 16, 1962, the trio went into the studios of a company called Radio Recorders in Hollywood, California. With Granz in his customary spot in the booth as the producer, Oscar, Brown, and Thigpen cut fifteen tunes. The album wasn't intended as anything special, just a straight-ahead swinging session. But as things developed, the trio hit a magnificent groove.

Their version of the title song, "Night Train," set the tone for the entire album. "Night Train" had begun in 1940 as a Duke Ellington composition, which he called "That's the Blues, Old Man." A few years later, Ellington showed his affection for the song by rerecording it under the fetching new title of "Happy Go Lucky Local." In 1951, a former Ellington tenor saxophonist named Jimmy Forrest recorded the song under yet another title – "Night Train." Forrest gave the tune a rhythm-and-blues treatment. His funky approach found popularity with the record-buying public. Jimmy Forrest's "Night Train" was a best-selling hit.

Oscar's version of the tune was more Ellington than Forrest, but not by much. The trio made "Night Train" into an ambling, infectious number, taken at medium tempo. Thigpen and Brown put down a flowing beat for Oscar, a rhythm that persuaded more than it pushed. Oscar reacted with a solo that seemed to spring from a rare mood of complete ease.

For the other tunes on the album, Oscar let himself go happily wherever they carried him. The songs included three more Ellington-related compositions, a Charlie Parker number, a collection of standards, and, as an afterthought, the uplifting song of Oscar's own, "Hymn to Freedom."

When *Night Train* was released early the following year, it became and remained Oscar's all-time best-selling album.

In the late spring of 1962, Norman Granz had had another of his frequent brainstorms.

Earlier in Oscar's career, he had recorded collections of songs from the composers whose work was catalogued in the Great American Songbook. The composers included such masters of popular music as George Gershwin, Richard Rodgers, and Jerome Kern. They wrote most of their songs, which were largely timeless love ballads, for Broadway stage shows. Oscar recorded several albums of these men's show tunes, each album devoted to a different composer.

Granz's 1962 proposal, brilliant in his opinion, was for the trio to rerecord every song by Gershwin, Rodgers, and the other composers on every Great American Songbook album that Oscar had recorded. The motivation wasn't to see what fresh inspiration Ed Thigpen could draw out of Oscar, though that would be a bonus. Granz had something more commercial in mind.

The earlier albums were recorded in basic monaural sound. Since then, stereo sound had arrived in all its glory. Stereo on records produced much crisper and more intimate sound, allowing listeners to imagine that they were right there in the studio alongside the musicians. Albums on stereo sold like hotcakes, and Granz wanted Oscar to take advantage of the new market with rerecordings of the songbook albums.

For a month that spring, the trio was booked into Chicago's London House. During ten days of the booking, Granz took

Oscar, Brown, and Thigpen into a studio to record. By night, the three worked the London House; by day, they recorded an astounding total of 117 tracks.

On the recordings, the trio produced little in the way of terrific jazz. But that was by design. On Granz's insistence, Oscar stuck mainly to playing the melody two or three times on each track. He left out the passages of improvisation he would normally add. Granz's reasoning was that the albums were aimed at stereo fans who likely knew little about jazz. Maybe the albums would make them into Oscar Peterson fans, as long as the music wasn't too intricate. "Keep things simple," Granz instructed Oscar. And Oscar served up the straight-ahead treatments the boss asked for.

Uninspired as the music was in jazz terms, the ten days of recording still presented yet another demonstration of Oscar's incredible stamina. No pianist in the history of jazz cut as many recordings of such variety as Oscar managed in his career in the music business.

He recorded with practically everybody with a jazz connection: with Louis Armstrong, jazz's original genius; with Charlie Parker, the musician who overturned much of what Armstrong represented in jazz; with every eminent alto saxophonist of the era, from the elegant Benny Carter to the blistering bebopper Sonny Stitt. He recorded with all the significant tenor saxophonists, from Lester Young to the next generation of tenors who idolized Young and based their early styles on his. "My kiddies," Young called younger stars like Stan Getz and Zoot Sims. On records, Oscar was equally confident with the master and with his kiddies.

———

From time to time, Oscar recorded duets – just him and one other musician – with no rhythm section and no other instruments. Count Basie was Oscar's partner in one two-piano duet and Duke Ellington in another. In a tour de force with the guitarist Joe Pass, Oscar recorded ten songs from the folk opera *Porgy and Bess*, by George and Ira Gershwin.

Of all his duet recordings, Oscar thought the most demanding came in the 1970s, when he made five two-man albums with five different trumpet players, one trumpet per album. The trumpeters included two swing era players, Roy Eldridge and Harry Edison; Clark Terry, who bridged a couple of jazz styles; Dizzy Gillespie, the bebop master; and a young protégé of Gillespie's named Jon Faddis. Out of his depth in such fast company, Faddis needed propping up on his record. He got it from Oscar. In later years, Oscar was pleased to see the once-faltering Faddis blossom into a powerful soloist.

The challenge from the other four trumpeters was different. Each player entered the studio ripe for battle with Oscar. They would go head-to-head, matching improvisations with him and seeing who came out ahead. But that wasn't what Oscar wanted. He was as competitive as any jazz musician, but on the trumpet sessions, he was looking for cooperation and empathy. The recordings wouldn't exactly be lovefests, but if Oscar had his way, calm assurance was what would ring through to the listeners.

As Oscar laid on his message in the studio, his manner and his playing disarmed each of the trumpeters. Oscar had other responsibilities on his mind. He needed to provide the rhythmic drive and the harmonic underpinnings that a full rhythm section would normally supply. But mostly he concentrated on getting the trumpet players into his own mood of sharing. The trumpet players soon wised up to what Oscar was all about.

They played so beautifully that an album from the trumpet sessions won a Grammy for Oscar in 1979, the fifth of his nine Grammies. This Grammy went to a composite album that brought together tracks from each of the trumpet sessions. All the trumpet players, Jon Faddis included, were likewise honored with Grammies for their playing on the difficult but extraordinarily rewarding albums.

Oscar also recorded with a generation of jazz singers. Most were female, though Louis Armstrong said he loved singing on records with Oscar behind him. Ella Fitzgerald was Oscar's most frequent vocal sidekick. She thrived alongside Oscar. And so did such other remarkable jazz singers as Sarah Vaughan, Anita O'Day, and Billie Holiday.

In a 1954 album, Oscar accompanied himself on vocals. A listener might at first have mistaken Oscar's singing voice for Nat Cole's. Oscar had a sound like Cole's and the same intimacy, but he was much less authoritative, as if his heart wasn't committed to the singing.

Oscar made a second vocal album, recorded in 1965, not long after Cole died of lung cancer. The album, titled *With Respect to Nat*, was devoted to songs that had been popular hits for Cole. Oscar's voice continued to sound much like his idol's. But Oscar still didn't seem to have his heart in it. He never cut another vocal album.

The most surprising vocalist Oscar accompanied on record was the great singer and dancer from Broadway and the movies, Fred Astaire. Astaire, not at all a temperamental star, was in awe of

Oscar and the other five jazz musicians on the recording date.

"Was that okay?" he would ask anxiously, after most takes. "Did I stay in tune?"

As well as contributing his voice to the recordings, Astaire added his feet. Performing on a mini dance floor rigged in the studio, Astaire tap-danced, matching his percussive steps to the beat of the rhythm section. He didn't need to ask anyone in the studio if his dancing was okay. Nobody danced like Fred Astaire.

The jazz experience pleased Astaire so much that he presented Oscar and the other five musicians with inscribed gold identification bracelets. Oscar put his on his right wrist and rarely took it off for the next several years. Astaire later told Oscar that he watched Oscar's appearances on TV, always checking to make sure he was wearing the bracelet. Astaire was never disappointed.

In the early spring of 1969, Oscar arrived at the A&R Studios in New York City to record with a large string orchestra. It was to be one of twelve albums Oscar made with string accompaniment over the course of his career. The 1969 album, titled *Motions & Emotions*, was notable for the high quality of the music and for the tantrum that Oscar threw in the studio.

At the time, Norman Granz was between record labels. He took no part in the financing and distribution of *Motions & Emotions*. Instead, the person behind the album was a wealthy German businessman named Hans Georg Brunner-Schwer, who owned MPS Records.

For Oscar, the key attraction in recording the album was Claus Ogerman, a German-born, New York City-based arranger of immense ingenuity. The plan was for Ogerman to write the arrangements for *Motions & Emotions* and conduct the orchestra in the studio. He came to the assignment with sterling credentials from both the pop and the jazz worlds. Having scored hit tunes for such massive pop stars as Leslie Gore, the Drifters, and Connie Francis, he'd also written orchestral arrangements for albums by luminous jazz artists like Stan Getz and the pianist Bill Evans. For Oscar, Ogerman prepared arrangements of mainly contemporary popular songs. Oscar knew he was in for a treat. He got excited just reading and humming the charts Ogerman had written.

In his album *Night Child*, Oscar wrote and played songs that described in music the joy and despair he felt over his son Joel. Shown on the album's cover, Joel was born in 1979, during Oscar's brief marriage to his third wife, Charlotte Huber.

Oscar, Ogerman, and everybody else assembled in the A&R Studios for the recording. The musicians were in their chairs, Ogerman stood at the podium, the engineers in the booth fiddled the sound to the right levels. Everybody was ready to roll. Everybody except Oscar. He looked at the piano and went into shock.

"I don't like the box," he said. "Box" was Oscar's name for a piano.

Oscar had ordered a particular grand piano made by the Baldwin piano company for the *Motions & Emotions* session. But the piano in the A&R Studios wasn't a Baldwin. Nor was it grand. Someone had messed up the piano delivery.

"What's going on, Oscar?" Ogerman asked.

"I'm done," Oscar answered. "I'm not playing this piano."

Now it was Brunner-Schwer's turn to go into shock. No matter what happened at A&R that day, he had to pay for the studio rental, for Ogerman's arrangements, and for the musicians' time, whether they played or not.

Brunner-Schwer faced an expensive dilemma. But he wasn't a wealthy businessman for nothing; he knew his way out of tough financial spots. He proposed to everyone at A&R that Ogerman record the string orchestra in the studio, then Oscar would record his piano sections over the tapes of the strings in a later session. Brunner-Schwer added that he knew just the piano that Oscar could play for the second recording. It wasn't a Baldwin, but it was an equally superb German Steinway at Brunner-Schwer's mansion in the small German city of Villingen. Oscar had played on this very piano a year earlier in Germany.

Brunner-Schwer's plan rescued the recording. Ogerman conducted the orchestra through the score at the A&R Studios.

Oscar performed his piano overdubbing at Villingen. And *Motions & Emotions* emerged as a gorgeous piece of work.

Claus Ogerman's arrangements transformed the familiar pop tunes into surprising new vehicles for Oscar's swing and imagination. He played three Beatles songs (his first and last Beatles recording session). In Oscar's and Ogerman's hands, "Yesterday" emerged as a samba, and "Eleanor Rigby" turned into blues.

Oscar soared through "This Guy's in Love with You," "Ode to Billy Joe," "Sunny," and several more pop hits of the 1960s. On this album, Oscar didn't float over top of the strings the way he did on his other "strings" albums. On *Motions & Emotions,* he worked in collaboration with the strings. They operated in counterpoint to one another. On "Sunny," Ogerman's arrangement allowed Oscar to throw some swinging passages at the strings. On "Ode to Billie Joe," Oscar got low-down and funky in his solo. The funk wasn't necessarily his idea; it was what Ogerman's strings suggested to him.

Oscar was overjoyed to work with Ogerman's arrangements. When he made *Motions & Emotions* in 1969, it was only the third time he had recorded with a string orchestra. He anticipated that Ogerman had set the pattern for future recordings with strings, but as Oscar's experience with string orchestras unfolded, nothing was ever again as dazzling as *Motions & Emotions.*

Oscar didn't collaborate with Ogerman a second time. Nor did he ever climb as high in quality with other orchestral arrangers. Most of the rest of Oscar's string experiences resulted in merely hip background music. Oscar plus strings came to mean easy listening with a jazz twist.

———

Back in the early 1960s, Oscar had a reason for taking a break from recording and performing. Like his father and his two sisters, Oscar liked to teach, instruct, evaluate, correct, criticize, and enlighten. "I get sick of listening to young musicians who make so many mistakes," he once complained.

As a way to reduce the population of bumbling jazz musicians, Oscar started a music school in Toronto in January 1960. Ray Brown and Ed Thigpen were two of his partners in the risky enterprise, but a key contributor was the Toronto composer and clarinetist Phil Nimmons, whose wife had been the inspiration for Oscar's "Noreen's Nocturne."

The school grew out of discussions among Oscar, Nimmons, and a few others to address the question *Why can't we teach people to play good jazz?* They hoped that one answer lay in their Advanced School of Contemporary Music.

Oscar found plenty of music to smile over in his 1980s trio, with Joe Pass on guitar and Niels Pedersen on bass.

ASCM's teaching staff included Brown, Thigpen, Oscar, and Nimmons. It was Nimmons who handled the classes in arranging and composition. The majority of students enrolled for piano with Oscar. He made sure the piano players also took lessons from Brown, on the reasonable premise that a pianist needed to know how to play cooperatively with a bassist. If a student showed up looking for lessons on trumpet or trombone or saxophone, the school recruited high-caliber local jazz musicians as part-time teachers.

A term at ASCM lasted six months and included sessions where students and staff sat around listening to jazz records. After each record, the staff proceeded to deconstruct the music they'd just heard. Oscar, who relished the chance to lecture about jazz's technical side, was the most frequently heard voice in the deconstruction exercises. Many students found these listening adventures as enlightening as the regular instrumental classes.

The students – about sixty signed up for each term, a significant number from the United States – were expected to arrive with acceptable facility on their instruments and some experience playing in bands. Most students did better than that; over fifty percent were professional musicians earning paychecks, though not necessarily in jazz. What they expected of Oscar and his fellow teachers was the knowledge that would get them over the creative hump. They hoped to leave the school with increased chances of becoming full-time jazz musicians.

Many graduates had their hopes come true. Such excellent Canadian pianists as Carol Britto, Doug Riley, and Wray Downes studied under Oscar at ASCM. The most accomplished of all the piano grads was undoubtedly Mike Longo of Fort Lauderdale,

Florida. Twenty-two years old when he took Oscar's classes, Longo already had a small reputation as the whiz kid who had played in his teenage years with a band led by the charismatic alto saxophonist Julian "Cannonball" Adderley.

A couple of decades after graduation from ASCM, when Longo was asked what he learned from Oscar, he answered, "Textures, voicings, touch, time, conception, tone on the instrument. In other words, just about everything." Longo kept up a solid career in jazz, working for long periods as Dizzy Gillespie's pianist and arranger. He grew so closely associated with Gillespie that he was asked to deliver a eulogy at the great trumpet player's funeral in 1993.

Finding and financing a locale for ASCM brought money problems. At the beginning, Oscar took the operation through two locations. Both were too small, and one, a really tight squeeze for a full complement of students, was Oscar's own house. Eventually the school settled in a large former rooming house at 21 Park Road, in midtown Toronto. It provided relative stability, but Oscar was already beginning to feel ASCM slipping away.

It was an awkward time for Oscar. Since the obligations he, Brown, and Thigpen owed to the students kept them from going on the road for long periods, they cut way back on concerts and club dates. Each of them missed the excitement of the trio's regular gigs.

To fill in the gap, Oscar often invited Brown and Thigpen to his house for nighttime sessions all by themselves. "Some of the best playing I've ever done," Oscar told Gene Lees, "was down in the basement with Ray and Ed."

But the jamming in the cellar was only a pleasant pause in Oscar's suddenly worry-filled life. He needed money to finance the school if he expected to keep it in business. He needed more money to help in his marriage crisis. Something had to give, and it was ASCM. In its fourth year of operation, 1964, the school offered just two months of classes. ASCM, sputtering toward collapse, closed its doors for good at the end of the year.

That was the signal for Oscar to return his professional life to its normal hectic pace. Although he thought his brief teaching career was valuable, Oscar most cherished his onstage career, playing the piano in concert halls and nightclubs. He put himself, Ray Brown, and Ed Thigpen on a full-time touring schedule, telling everyone who came to hear them how good it felt to be back.

CHAPTER ELEVEN

OSCAR'S TOYS AND PASTIMES

hen Oscar had time off from jazz, he went for activities that involved gadgets. Sports weren't his style; he just wasn't an athletic kind of guy. In the 1950s, he bought a set of golf clubs thinking he would take up the game, but all he got for his troubles were cysts on his wrists, causing him much pain. He worried they might affect his piano playing. When the cysts eventually cleared up, Oscar swore he'd never swing another golf club.

He had far better success with fly casting, an activity that called for skill with a gadget – in this case, a fly rod. To Oscar's way of thinking, fly casting was at least as much art as sport.

For Oscar, the serious connection to fly rods began when he purchased his summer place in Haliburton. Not long afterwards, Oscar and his trio were playing a long engagement at Ronnie Scott's, the number-one jazz club in London, England. He learned that a shop named Hardy's, established in 1872 in the chic Pall Mall section of the city, specialized in the very best fishing equipment and clothing. Oscar spent a small fortune in the store. While he was at it, he took the unusual step of hiring the Hardy's salesman, an accommodating fellow named Scotty, for lessons in fly casting.

Over several days, Oscar rose at dawn, still groggy from a long night at Ronnie Scott's. Together, he and Scotty drove to a river just outside London, where Scotty gave Oscar instructions in the fine art of casting his fishing rod.

Oscar polished his skills, and for years, fly-fishing in his cherished Haliburton lakes remained the one activity he could count on for releasing the stresses of his jazz life.

A spelling bee in grade four brought Oscar to the most addictive of his nonmusical passions, when a small Kodak camera was put up as the prize. Oscar wanted that camera more than anything in his young life, and the competition was stiff.

Not normally keen on homework, Oscar studied for the spelling bee like a boy possessed. When the bee ended, Oscar was the last kid standing. He won the camera, and with it, he launched a lifelong love affair with photography and all the accompanying gadgets.

––––––

For years, Oscar was content with the little Kodak. But as jazz success and money came his way, he spent lavishly on cameras and photographic equipment. He set up a darkroom at home, where he developed his own photographs, edited them, cropped them, and enlarged them.

Since he couldn't bear the thought of leaving photography behind when he went on the road, Oscar devised a portable darkroom to accompany him around the world. He packed developing chemicals, a miniature enlarger, and all the rest of a photographer's tools. When the concerts and club dates finished at night, Oscar rushed back to the improvised darkrooms in the bathrooms of his hotel suites. While the other musicians found adventures – and sometimes trouble – in bars and clubs, Oscar had time only for his enthralling hobby.

In the daytime on the road, Oscar wandered the streets of whatever city he was performing in with two or three cameras slung over his shoulder. Early on, he worked with German Leicas, then switched to Swedish Hasselblads. He taught himself how all his cameras worked through his technical instincts, only bothering to read camera manuals as a last resort. He was a natural at photography and its mechanics. When digital cameras came along, it was a smooth transition for Oscar to the Canon 1D and the Fuji S2.

As his subject matter, Oscar shot buildings, especially during his trips to Europe, with its beautiful old cities. His hero was Henri Cartier-Bresson, the great French photographer regarded as the father of photojournalism. Oscar and Cartier-Bresson differed in one fundamental; Cartier-Bresson worked in black and white while Oscar preferred color.

Oscar fastened on to Cartier-Bresson's observation that "a photograph could fix eternity in a moment." What Oscar liked shooting the most, what he tried to fix for eternity were faces. He photographed faces in the street, particularly those of the very young and the very old. When he saw an engaging face, he clicked away with his camera. This explained why the shelves and drawers in Oscar's library at home were filled with hundreds of photographs of complete strangers.

Though disease had partly crippled Oscar's left hand, he still played with the old fire in his performance at the 1995 Montreal Jazz Festival. His quartet included the Toronto guitarist Lorne Lofsky.

Oscar's occupation, jazz musician, required the biggest of all the gadgets that filled his life. What was larger, more dominant, more beautiful, and harder to master than a piano? Nothing that Oscar could think of. And yet it took years of searching before he owned a piano that he could call the best in the world.

During his childhood, Oscar made do with the two pianos he played at home in St. Henri. The first was the cheap, black upright piano his father leased for the family. The next, a marginal improvement, was purchased secondhand with the $250.00 in prize money that fifteen-year-old Oscar won in the CBC-Radio amateur music contest. The idea of the purchase was Daniel Peterson's, and like the first piano, the second was placed at the service of all the Petersons.

Oscar didn't get a superior piano of his own until the early 1950s, a few years after he and Lil moved into a Montreal apartment. By then, largely through JATP, Oscar's reputation as a pianist was on a swift rise. Everybody knew his name, including the clerk in the piano department at Eaton's department store in down-town Montreal. Oscar wanted a grand piano made by Steinway & Sons, the world's most prominent maker of superb pianos.

As Oscar often told the story, the Eaton's clerk got on the phone to make several calls. Then he turned to Oscar. "Mr. Peterson, Steinways asked if you would allow Mr. Steinway himself to send you the piano he'd like you to have."

In telling the anecdote, Oscar never filled in crucial names and details. Who, for example, was "Mr. Steinway himself"? Oscar didn't say, but it was probably Henry Z. Steinway, the great grand-son of the man who started Steinway & Sons in 1853, with operations in Hamburg, Germany, and in New York City. A century later, though Henry Z. was one among several male Steinways in the family business, he ran the three piano-making factories in New York City's Queens borough. Henry Z., or perhaps one of his senior advisors, was savvy enough to realize that Oscar Peterson could give Steinway some excellent public relations.

Three months after Oscar's visit to Eaton's, a Steinway grand was delivered to the Peterson apartment. Oscar was impressed beyond words by what he called the piano's "luminosity and richness of tone." He and the Steinway people got together on a deal: Oscar would endorse Steinway products, and in return, Steinway would provide its very best grand pianos for Oscar's North American concerts and nightclub dates.

It was an arrangement that Steinway historically signed with the world's famous pianists. Over time, they ranged from the great classical genius Vladimir Horowitz to pop music's Billy Joel and jazz's Diana Krall. In the 1950s, Oscar knew that his agreement with Steinway was another sign of his arrival in the big time.

In 1957, playing a concert with his trio at a hall in Copenhagen, Denmark, Oscar couldn't believe that the hall's piano was as exquisite as it felt and sounded. Thirty minutes after the concert ended, he sneaked back into the hall, which he thought was now empty. Oscar sat at the piano and played long enough to satisfy himself that the piano really was close to heaven.

"You like it?" asked a man half-hidden at the side of the stage, introducing himself as an executive at a local piano maker. "I've got a warehouse full of pianos like this one. Come around tomorrow, and you'll see."

In the warehouse next day, Oscar tested several pianos, settling on a Danish-made, ebony-colored Hornung & Moeller as his favorite. As the man said, it sounded just like the piano Oscar played the night before.

"It's yours, a gift from us," the man went on, saying he'd even pay for the shipping charges to Oscar's house. All he asked in return was a photograph of Oscar and a little note saying he liked the piano.

Oscar put the new Hornung & Moeller in the basement recreation room at the Peterson house in Toronto, where the family moved in 1958. He practiced on the piano for hours, and he had fun showing off the marvelous instrument to his friends.

Then things went wrong. The piano wouldn't stay in tune. Oscar kept calling on his piano tuner to restore the Hornung & Moeller, but each time, the piano would soon lose its tuning again. Oscar decided that Toronto's weather was at fault: too dry or too damp, too oppressive for the lovely piano. Oscar sold the Hornung & Moeller to a friend who thought he could overcome Toronto's unwelcoming attitude to the precious piano's tuning.

Oscar knew that pianists, of all musicians, were engaged in a perpetual battle.

"There's one thing I hate about being a pianist," he said. "Other musicians play the same instrument every night. But we have to take what we're given, pianos of all shapes and sizes, in tune and out of tune, with tight keys or loose keys, with pedals that work or don't work the right way."

The point of Oscar's deal with Steinway was to guarantee that he played acceptable pianos. But Steinway sometimes failed to live up to its promises. Oscar couldn't put his finger on the nature of Steinway's problem, but by the mid-1960s, the company's delivery system seemed to have broken down. Pianos were delayed in arriving at concert halls and clubs. Often the pianos failed to show up at all. Oscar was left scrambling for substitutes.

At about the same time, a Cincinnati friend of Oscar's who worked for the Baldwin piano company persuaded Oscar to take a long look at Baldwin's new SD-10 grand piano. Baldwin had been founded in Cincinnati in 1857, the largest purely American maker of pianos. For years, Oscar hadn't cared for the Baldwin. He thought the tone felt cold, and there was something a little off in the action of the keys. But the new version, the SD-10 grand, produced a warm tone, the keys responding just the way Oscar wanted them to. This Baldwin swept him away.

Oscar ended his deal with Steinway, agreeing that Baldwin would supply the pianos for his North American gigs and recordings. The competition among piano makers was sometimes fierce, and each company tried to outshine the others in the caliber of the pianists who endorsed its product.

Baldwin already had an impressive roster. It included the classical conductor and composer Leonard Bernstein, the colorful pianist and TV host Liberace, and the jazzman Dave Brubeck. Oscar joined the Baldwin list in an arrangement that lasted ten years. Then Oscar moved on to something he considered even better, never resting in his search for the most satisfying piano.

In mid-1963, when Oscar accepted an invitation to play for a small private party in Germany, he had no way of knowing that the event would lead him to the most wonderful piano of his life nor that it would bring about the best recordings he ever made.

At the time of the invitation, Oscar and his trio – Ray Brown and Ed Thigpen – were in the middle of a European tour, booked as usual by Norman Granz. One concert was in the Swiss city of Zurich. The man who wanted Oscar's trio to play at the private gathering lived not far from Zurich, across the Swiss border in a small German city called Villingen. It would be a tight squeeze to fit the new booking into the few hours after the Zurich concert, but the man seemed unusually persistent. And he didn't blink an eye when Granz asked him to pay Oscar's full fee plus expenses.

The host with the deep pockets was Hans Georg Brunner-Schwer, the businessman who later financed Oscar's strings album with Claus Ogerman. *Motions & Emotions* was just one of several Oscar recordings that Brunner-Schwer would bankroll over the years.

Brunner-Schwer's family fortune came from the manufacture of radio receivers. Hans Georg himself had passions for both sound and jazz. To him, these were no idle pursuits. He backed his enthusiasm with loads of money spent in equipping his mansion with the most up-to-date audio equipment.

At the Villingen mansion, Oscar thought he had arrived for the private concert in a paradise. Sitting at the excellent Hamburg Steinway piano in the mansion's living room, Oscar's view through the huge picture window took in a vista of immaculate lawns crisscrossed by orderly gardeners' paths. Beds of roses surrounded the lawns on all sides. And far beyond the roses, the trees of Germany's Black Forest towered along the horizon. In this setting, Oscar felt uplifted.

While Oscar, Brown, and Thigpen performed for the twenty-five or thirty guests in the living room, Brunner-Schwer retreated to his dream of a studio on the second floor. He had already placed six microphones in strategic arrangement around the three musicians in the living room. Then, on the second floor, with Oscar's approval, he manned the soundboard, pouring all his recording finesse into taping the music downstairs.

It was clear to the musicians that Brunner-Schwer was not just a committed jazz fan who happened to be wealthy. He also had a solid background in music. Like Oscar, Brunner-Schwer possessed perfect pitch. Like Oscar, he played the piano (though nothing remotely close to Oscar's level). And like Oscar, Brunner-Schwer understood the mechanics in the ongoing effort to reach recording perfection.

As soon as the concert at the mansion ended, Brunner-Schwer led Oscar upstairs to the studio, where he played the tapes of the evening's music. He had no intention of marketing an album; Brunner-Schwer's studio work was strictly for his own pleasure. But when Oscar listened to the music, he began to develop more ambitious ideas.

Oscar thought that few, if any, commercial studios could match the sound Brunner-Schwer produced in his home operation. And there was something else that surprised Oscar: He thought he sounded different on these tapes. He sounded the way his own ears heard the music when he was playing at his best.

"I know I'm going to be coming back to Villingen," Oscar told Brunner-Schwer.

Over the following eleven years, Oscar made fifteen albums in Brunner-Schwer's studio. These occasions at the mansion were social as well as musical. Oscar and his musicians stayed at the mansion, enjoying sumptuous meals and much conversation. Though Oscar thought Brunner-Schwer had a few puzzling

quirks in his makeup, he found the German millionaire fascinating when the two men discussed the technical secrets in the
search for matchless recorded sound.

In his midseventies, Oscar composed and played on an album of songs
evoking a few of his favorite cities, towns, and neighborhoods. The celebrated French composer and arranger Michel Legrand (center) wrote the
arrangements. (The man on the right was Legrand's musical assistant.)

During the eleven years of Villingen visits and on into the
succeeding years, the personnel in Oscar's groups shuffled
through significant changes. Ray Brown and Ed Thigpen left
the trio within a few months of one another in 1966. Thigpen
moved to Denmark, where he started a family and became a
major figure on the European jazz scene. Brown followed
Herb Ellis's example, settling into the Los Angeles commercial

music business. As Ellis did, Brown frequently took time off to revisit the jazz world, sometimes for concerts and recordings with Oscar.

For Oscar, the era of his powerful trios with fixed personnel had ended. He continued to play in trios and quartets, but now the musicians he chose to play with worked for him in shifting combinations. Since nobody would ever turn down a chance to play with Oscar, he had his pick of the very best bassists, guitarists, and drummers.

On guitar, a musician named Joe Pass emerged as preeminent in jazz in the 1960s. Oscar admired Pass's work on records, but he didn't come face-to-face with the man until a night in 1972, when Oscar dropped into a Los Angeles jazz club called Donte's. Pass was the feature attraction, working in a duo with a bass player. When Pass spotted Oscar in the audience, he invited him to join the two musicians onstage.

Oscar and Pass started off with the standard, "Just Friends." In no time, the music turned fast, competitive, and adventurous. Oscar caught fire from Pass. "Oh my," he said of the evening, "I found someone whose playing inspired me so intensely that I seemed to have reached a creative level that might have gone undiscovered without him."

For the next twenty years, Oscar regularly called on Pass for gigs and recordings. One trio session with Pass and a bassist, recorded live at Chicago's London House in May 1973, was so striking that it won a Grammy Award for Best Jazz Group of the Year.

"Joe Pass," Oscar said, "helped make me a better player."

———

The bassist on the Grammy-winning album was Niels-Henning Orsted Pedersen, a musician from Denmark. Oscar and Pedersen came together in 1971 under strange circumstances. On a tour of Europe with a trio that included the excellent Czech bassist George Mraz, Oscar was scheduled to play in the Croatian city of Zagreb. To the Croatians, people of Mraz's Czech background had long been regarded as mortal enemies. Mraz didn't dare accompany Oscar to Zagreb. It might cost him his life.

When Oscar sent out frantic calls for a substitute bassist, Norman Granz came up with Pedersen. Not familiar with the young bassist's work, Oscar approached the concert with caution. But after the first few tunes, Oscar realized that the Danish kid was a true bass virtuoso. Pedersen had a sure touch for melody, a large store of harmonic ideas, and he kept impeccable time. Who could ask for more?

Pedersen worked in the Peterson trio off and on for the next thirty years. Ray Brown said the young Dane was the only bassist in the business with the technique to match Oscar at top velocity. Oscar agreed. He thought Pedersen was superb.

When Oscar was asked to assess his bass players – to choose between Brown and Pedersen as the best bassist ever to play in the trio – he gave a diplomatic answer. He said the two were the top bass players he worked with, equally great but different.

On a steaming hot summer evening in mid-July 1977, Oscar performed a set of seven tunes at Switzerland's famous Montreux Jazz Festival. His unorthodox trio consisted of himself on piano plus the two bassists, Brown and Pedersen, onstage together for the first and possibly only time. The result was a sensation in which Oscar took second place to the bassists, who found inspiration in one another.

It wasn't hard to tell the two bass players apart on this night. Brown was the one with the fat tone and the pretty melodies. Pedersen had the speedy fingers and the musical lines that were clean as a whistle. Playing with the two, Oscar was as happy as anyone had ever seen him on a stage. In a film of the Montreux event, Oscar's smile never left his face.

Over the years, Oscar took Brown and Pedersen separately to Villingen to record under Hans Georg Brunner-Schwer's expert hand. Oscar recorded at Villingen with many of his favorite people – with Brown and Pedersen, with Joe Pass, Ed Thigpen, and Herb Ellis. Always the proud host, he invited other special guests to record there. One was Milt Jackson, the inventive vibraphonist in the Modern Jazz Quartet. More surprising were the four members of Singers Unlimited, three men and a woman named Bonnie Herman, who sang lead. The group didn't necessarily fit into the jazz category, but Oscar thought its uncanny harmonizing made Singers Unlimited exhilarating company.

Of all the outstanding recordings Oscar made at Villingen, the one that most thrilled him was called *My Favorite Instrument*. Oscar was a solo pianist; he had no company on the album, no sidemen, no rhythm section. He played a program of standard show tunes all by himself. The result was a different Oscar.

This Oscar took everything down a notch. Without losing spontaneity, he played a little less in every sense. There were fewer asides, fewer notes, not so much bravura work, and it was quieter in the emotions. Oscar was less interested in excitement and much more caught up in the pensive side of his personality. He played like a pianist who was reflecting on the music his fingers produced.

"I think *My Favorite Instrument* was the best album I've ever recorded," Oscar said a few years later. "Perhaps that was because it was the first album where I was completely free, and in which I did what I felt like. I chose the tempos and the keys I wanted to play in. If I wanted to change keys in the middle of a tune, there was no problem because I was alone at the piano with no other musicians to give me trouble."

Each time Oscar traveled to Villingen, his second wife, Sandy, went along. She accompanied Oscar on just about every trip he made away from home. Sandy had given up her nursing job, and partly because the couple had no children together and no one else to keep her at home, she hit the road alongside her husband.

Sandy loved visiting new and foreign places, but, most of all, she loved the music. When Sandy sat through Oscar's faraway performances, it didn't feel like a wifely duty. It felt like fun. Everybody in Oscar's jazz world came to know Sandy. She was hard to miss — a lively, active woman whose voice and laughter soared over practically everybody else's.

Sandy had an opinion on most subjects. So did Oscar. Both liked a good discussion, no matter what the topic was. With time — the two were together for close to two decades — the discussions began to turn into arguments that could last all day and much of the night. Later on, Oscar talked of noisy fights with Sandy that left him on the brink of exhaustion when stepping onstage.

Oscar's theory about Sandy and the quarrels centered on her background as an operating-room nurse. Without this important and consuming job, Sandy began to feel unfulfilled. It was nice to travel the world as the wife of the great Oscar Peterson, but she missed the thrill of personal accomplishment.

"Sandy became both envious and resentful," Oscar later wrote, "thinking of the career she had given up."

In 1974, Oscar was invited to perform in Russia. It was a time when the Cold War was keeping a deep freeze on relations between the Communist countries and the Western democracies. The invitation for a Canadian artist to play in Russia was a rare and important event. It had political as well as musical implications.

Oscar felt anxious over his role as an unofficial ambassador. It was no help to his mission when he and Sandy got into one of their screaming sessions during the tour. By the end of the time in Russia, Oscar was so upset with Sandy that he put her on a plane back to Canada while he continued to play concerts in other European cities. This ugly parting speeded the end of the marriage.

When Sandy divorced Oscar, she had been away from nursing for more than fifteen years – too late, in her opinion, to make up the lost time and return to her former profession. Instead, she took a job in the personnel department of Sears, her father's old employer. Once she and Oscar were separated, their friendship returned, and they stayed in touch. Sandy married again in 1987 and moved away from Toronto with her new husband.

Oscar's third marriage was to a Swissair flight attendant named Charlotte Huber. The couple met in 1977, when Oscar was once again playing a European concert tour. Though Charlie, as Oscar affectionately nicknamed Charlotte, was much younger than Oscar, the two fell into a romance. They were married in the large house in suburban Toronto's city of Mississauga, which Oscar had bought several years earlier. Not long afterwards, Charlie gave birth to a son, whom the couple named Joel.

Oscar adored Joel. He even managed to be at home for the baby's birth. But love for Joel wasn't enough to keep Charlie and Oscar together. Oscar later thought he had mistakenly married Charlie on the rebound from his broken relationship with Sandy. The inevitable breakup was, in Oscar's words, "sour and sardonic."

Charlie won custody of Joel, and she soon moved away from Toronto. Oscar rarely saw his son. Short as Oscar's time with Charlie turned out to be, he managed to compose and record a series of songs that covered the couple's brief years together. One song, titled simply "Charlie," evoked Charlotte's beauty and appeal. A tune Oscar named "Night Child" reflected on the birth of Joel, a baby who came in the night. And finally Oscar wrote "He Has Gone," a description in music of Oscar's feelings about losing his son to divorce and separation.

In July 1970, when Oscar recorded at Villingen with the Singers Unlimited, Brunner-Schwer had renovated his studio. The renovation included a change in pianos, replacing the German Steinway grand with a Bösendorfer Imperial. The Bösendorfer was an Austrian product, a brand of piano that Oscar had come across a few times over the years. The particular Bösendorfer at Villingen impressed Oscar, but it wasn't until a few years later that he fell head over heels in love with one.

In the meantime, Oscar's partnership with Brunner-Schwer hit the rocks. Though Oscar continued to find Brunner-Schwer a brilliant producer, he seemed very odd in his behavior. Once, when Brunner-Schwer invited Oscar and Sandy to another estate he owned on Lake Como, Italy, Oscar noticed that his host had decorated the grounds with several German Second World War air raid sirens. Among the sirens, he had placed a large-sized searchlight from the same war. Oscar and Sandy looked at one another, both thinking Brunner-Schwer was a weird guy.

Oscar could have lived with the weirdness, but what he couldn't stand was Brunner-Schwer's sniping at Norman Granz. When Brunner-Schwer complained to Oscar about Granz's business practices, Oscar listened patiently. But when Brunner-Schwer's remarks escalated into criticism of Granz's character, Oscar told him he had overstepped the bounds. Granz was Oscar's closest friend. With Oscar, friends came first. This difference of opinion led Oscar to cut off his connections with Brunner-Schwer. He never again recorded in the Villingen mansion.

In the late 1970s, Oscar played a concert in Vienna, Austria. When he finished, he raved to Granz about the wonders of that night's piano. It was a Bösendorfer. Word about Oscar's ecstatic reaction reached the ears of the Bösendorfer executives. They invited him to come to their offices and test some pianos.

Oscar was taken to a former monastery in the city, which served as Bösendorfer's manufacturing center. Oscar's bassist, Niels Pedersen, who played pretty good piano, went along on the tour. At the visit's climax, Oscar and Pedersen were escorted into a large room where twenty Bösendorfer pianos were on display. The pianos looked magnificent. As Oscar said, the Bösendorfers were presented in the showroom like "a herd of beautiful Arabian horses."

Oscar and Pedersen spent a blissful hour going their separate ways through the rows of pianos. They played each instrument, testing the keys, the tone, the pedals. Oscar couldn't make up his mind which piano was superior to the rest. Every piano felt like a wonder.

Then Pedersen hurried over to Oscar, telling him he should try this special piano in the room. Pedersen said he'd never heard any instrument as gorgeous as this. When Oscar sat down at the piano, placed his fingers on the keys, and played, he knew in an instant that Pedersen was right. The piano had a dark and pure tone. The sound seemed to sustain forever the richness of tone hanging in the air.

The piano that entranced Oscar was an Imperial 290. The company had poured all its resources and technology into the instrument. It had ninety-seven keys rather than the conventional eighty-eight. The additional keys opened up new possibilities for pianists, providing, among other treats, a low A with special resonance.

The 290 seemed to Oscar a giant among pianos, offering exactly the characteristics he looked for in an instrument. Bösendorfer's executives were as pleased with Oscar's choice as he was. They made a present to him of the mighty Imperial. It became the piano that Oscar played at home and at special Canadian concerts for the rest of his musical life.

When Oscar selected the piano, he knew little of Bösendorfer's history. The piano wizard who founded the company was Ignaz Bösendorfer of Vienna. He lived from 1794 to 1858, when his son Ludwig took over the business. While nineteenth-century pianists agreed that the Bösendorfer was a fine and worthy instrument, Bösendorfer sales didn't take off until one pianist in particular found that the Bösendorfer met all his needs. This pianist, noted for his powerful and impulsive playing technique, often found that most pianos lost their tone and pitch when he attacked them.

Then he came across the Bösendorfer – a piano that refused to buckle under his power. Adopting the Bösendorfer as his preferred piano, the pianist poured praise on the instrument, bringing it new fame. The Bösendorfer soon won a big chunk of the piano market, thanks to the pianist. That pianist was Franz Liszt.

If Oscar was, as Paul de Marky once said, "the jazz reincarnation of Franz Liszt," then he had at last found in the Bösendorfer the piano he was destined to play.

CHAPTER TWELVE

OSCAR'S COURAGE

B y the 1990s, it was nothing new for Oscar to receive another award. Hardly a month went by without a jazz organization, a college or university, or a branch of government inviting him to receive its recognition. Oscar was gracious about accepting each prize, though he had to admit that, as he entered his seventies, the ceremonies that went with the awards wore him down.

Nevertheless, Oscar was looking forward to the events

planned for Monday, May 10, 1993. That night, he was to receive the Glenn Gould Prize. Gould, the late concert pianist, was the only Canadian pianist besides Oscar whose fame reached around the world. In Gould's name, the Glenn Gould Foundation gave a prize of fifty thousand dollars every three years to an international artist who had made an essential contribution in music.

The violinist Yehudi Menuhin won the prize in 1990. Cellist Yo-Yo Ma would be the choice in 1999, followed by pianist-conductor André Previn in 2005 and singer-songwriter Leonard Cohen in 2011.

In 1993, Oscar was to join the illustrious company of Glenn Gould Prize winners.

The ceremony was scheduled for the Glenn Gould Studio in Toronto's CBC Building, not more than a dozen miles from Oscar's Mississauga home. The local flavor gave the prize special meaning for Oscar. But even more gratifying, his new wife and their little daughter would be in the audience.

After three failed marriages, Oscar had resolved never to marry again. But in the early 1980s, he met a young woman named Kelly Green in the lobby of a restaurant she managed in Sarasota, Florida. Kelly had a peaches and cream complexion, a perpetual smile, and plenty of good sense. Oscar was smitten, but he proceeded into the romance with care.

Kelly had no such reservations, even though Oscar was thirty years her senior. When she began dating Oscar, Kelly said, "I got lucky."

Oscar's friends adored her. "Why don't you ask Kelly to marry you?" Norman Granz said to Oscar at lunch one day. As he had many times before, Oscar took Granz's advice. When Kelly answered his proposal with a yes, Granz threw the wedding party. In his customary style, he went first-class all the way. The marriage ceremony was held in a suite at the elegant L'Ermitage Hotel in Beverly Hills, California, and the reception was at Chasen's, Hollywood's restaurant to the stars.

If the late marriage came as a surprise to Oscar, the birth in the summer of 1991 of his seventh child, a daughter named Celine, produced even greater unexpected joy. On the day of Celine's birth, Oscar was on a three-week European tour booked many months earlier. Although he missed the birth, for the first and only time with any of his children, Oscar was home to watch Celine take her first steps.

To make sure he had a part in the rest of his new daughter's major moments, Oscar took Kelly and Celine on all his road trips. Traveling with his family was another first for Oscar.

In the early 1990s, thanks to Kelly and Celine, Oscar was in top mental and emotional health. Physically, he was a wreck.

Arthritis, the disease that afflicted the Peterson family, didn't pass Oscar by. His fingers, which often gave him terrible pain when he was a young man, hurt even more in his advancing years. He struggled not to allow the arthritis to affect his playing.

In 1992, he needed to take time away from the piano to undergo two hip-replacement surgeries. Lying in bed in Toronto's Orthopedic and Arthritic Hospital, Oscar wondered if the time had come for him to give up the grueling life of the on-the-road jazz musician. It was tempting to spare himself all the exhausting travel, all the airports, hotels, and restaurants.

But the allure of performing for audiences remained as irresistible as ever. He would keep on playing, and he would keep on traveling, even though the hip operations meant he needed a walker or wheelchair to get around.

In the spring of 1993, Oscar put together a quartet of his favorite players: Ray Brown, Herb Ellis, and a young drummer named Jeff Richmond. Accompanied by Kelly and Celine, Oscar's quartet toured Japan for three weeks. Shaking off the rust, Oscar hit a comfortable pace. It was just like old times.

From Japan, Oscar and his family flew home to Toronto for a short rest. Then everybody gathered in New York City, where the quartet had a weekend date to play at a jazz hot spot called the Blue Note Club. On the following Monday, Oscar would accept the Glenn Gould Prize.

On Saturday night, at the end of the first two sets at the Blue Note, the quartet finished things off with "Blues Etude," a hard swinging tune Oscar had written. The song's climax featured a fast boogie-woogie passage.

On this night, Oscar fumbled the boogie-woogie. He couldn't seem to get the fingers of his left hand around the notes. The same thing happened on the same tune at the end of the second set. Oscar had been playing boogie-woogie since he was a kid at Montreal High. How could he bungle the boogie-woogie?

"What's happening, man?" Ray Brown asked, puzzled and worried.

Kelly wanted to call a doctor.

Oscar waved off the idea. He was just a little tired. That was all.

Back home in Toronto on Monday morning, Oscar hurried to the Glenn Gould Studio for a rehearsal of the evening's events. Governor-General Raymond Hnatyshyn was going to present the Glenn Gould Prize, Oscar would play a couple of tunes, and CBC Radio would broadcast the entire ceremony.

That night, Oscar played well and looked suitably grateful for the high honor. He got through the evening, but unknown to everybody except himself and Kelly, he was barely holding on.

"When he came home that night," Kelly said, "it was really obvious something serious was wrong."

Oscar had suffered a stroke. It probably hit him in New York City, at the time he stumbled on "Blues Etude." The effects of the stroke worsened, inflicting damage to the left side of Oscar's body. His left hand was especially weakened.

In hospital, Oscar began the process of recovery. The rehab was slow, tedious, and painful. For a creative artist like Oscar, it was a frightening experience to lose so many of his powers.

"I went into a sort of morass," Oscar wrote of the depression that flattened him.

Things grew so rough that Oscar spoke of getting rid of his piano – the ultimate sign of hopelessness. If he could even imagine life without the Bösendorfer, Oscar was on the edge of surrendering to his disease.

Then Dave Young phoned.

———

Young was a Canadian bassist who worked in both branches of music – jazz and classical. He was the principal bassist in the Hamilton Symphony Orchestra, and in his jazz life, he accompanied an impressive list of top pianists. In 1975, he was offered a position as the Winnipeg Symphony Orchestra's principal bassist. Simultaneously, Oscar asked Young to tour with him in Asia. Dave chose Oscar over the symphony.

For years afterwards, Young continued to get plenty of work in both jazz and symphonic music. He kept up his connection with Oscar, and when he heard about his friend's health problems, he called to insist that he and Oscar get together to jam a little. Oscar said he didn't think it was a good idea. Ignoring Oscar's doubts, Young showed up at the Mississauga house with his bass. Dave sensed that even Kelly felt he was on a doomed mission.

But the two men went to the music room in the basement. Oscar sat at the Bösendorfer, and they began to play. They led off with "Love Ballade," a tune of Oscar's that he performed frequently in the years just before his stroke.

"Oscar was kind of disappointed with his playing," Young said of the session. "But he was interested. It was as if he was thinking, *Maybe this will work.*"

Young and Oscar played together two or three more times. The basement get-togethers turned out to be enough to kick-start Oscar. Thoughts of getting rid of the Bösendorfer disappeared. Oscar was back in business.

Oscar's left hand never recovered its former strength and mobility. The right hand did most of the work, with contributions from the left that were careful and limited. But as one of Oscar's admirers said, "Moderation suited him now." He wasn't the hard-driving player he used to be, but there was no quit in Oscar. He continued to hit a pace that made his listeners feel good.

Nor was his essential style lost to the stroke. He mixed up bop and blues and whatever else occurred to him, just as he always had. His playing was a touch lighter, from the right hand as well as the left. But he wasn't slow with his improvisations; he was still the musician with the quick mind, even if the hands weren't always as swift in picking up the ideas.

Oscar assembled a new quartet. It was made up of his longtime sidekick Niels Pedersen on bass, the drummer Martin Drew, and a relative newcomer named Ulf Wakenius playing guitar. Pedersen, Drew, and Wakenius were from, respectively, Denmark, England, and Sweden. Oscar nicknamed his group the United Nations Quartet.

The quality Oscar said he most admired in the three musicians was exuberance. But they had a lot more going for them than just energy and razzle-dazzle. The three men showed as much musicianship as any players among Oscar's half-century of sidemen.

The UN group provided the backing in late 1994, when Oscar recorded his duets with the classical violinist Itzhak Perlman. They accompanied him on several return engagements at the Blue Note in New York. And with the UN people, Oscar once again joined a string orchestra in a 2000 recording.

For this album titled *Trail of Dreams*, Oscar wrote a series of short pieces evoking parts of the Canadian landscape. They were slight tunes with cute titles like "Banff the Beautiful" and

"Manitoba Minuet." The well-known French composer, pianist, and conductor Michel Legrand arranged the material and conducted the musicians in the studio. Legrand knew jazz and how to present *Trail of Dreams* in a hip jazz wrapping. The music wasn't profound, but it had plenty of sparkle.

In the early years of the twenty-first century, Oscar took time in concerts and club dates to talk to audiences about his jazz friends who were slipping away. It must have been painful for Oscar to list the names. But he insisted on asking everybody to remember Norman Granz, who died in 2001. Oscar's great bene-factor was gone. So was his magnificent bassist, Ray Brown, who died in his sleep while he was on the road for a jazz gig in 2002. Oscar's other remarkable bassist, Niels Pedersen, died in 2005. There were more, but Oscar usually ended the list with John Lewis, the pianist and composer for the Modern Jazz Quartet and a good friend to Oscar. Lewis died in 2001.

Oscar would follow the listing of names by playing a slow, sweet tune he wrote not long after Lewis's death. Oscar called it "Requiem."

There was one death that he never spoke of onstage and found almost impossible to mention in private. It was the passing from kidney disease in 2002 of his second daughter, Sharon.

On June 8, 2007, Oscar was invited as a special guest to a jazz concert in Carnegie Hall. His appearance there held all sorts of personal significance. Carnegie was, of course, the venue where he had first performed in the United States. He'd been a special guest on that occasion too. It had taken place fifty-seven years earlier. Oscar wondered where the years had gone.

At the 2007 concert, Oscar would be in the company of many of his surviving piano contemporaries. Most of them were even older than Oscar. Hank Jones, a pianist of effortless technique, was eighty-eight. Billy Taylor, a fluid and inventive bop-inclined player, was eighty-four. The elegant and intelligent Marian McPartland was eighty-six. Freddie Cole, Nat's younger brother and uncannily like Nat in his vocals and piano playing, was the kid of the group at seventy-four.

But Oscar hadn't the strength for travel and for the Carnegie concert. The Peterson family was represented in the audience that night by Kelly and Celine, and the concert made a point of honoring Oscar. While his fellow octogenarians, along with Freddie Cole, played, Oscar stayed home.

A little later that June, Oscar couldn't rally himself for an appearance at the annual Toronto Jazz Festival. His playing days seemed over. For decades, he had managed to stay the course through diseases that were frightening in their number. He'd survived childhood tuberculosis, arthritis, high blood pressure, hip replacements, heart disease, and at least one stroke.

In the end, he was overcome by liver failure. Oscar died on a Sunday night at home in Mississauga: December 23, 2007. He was eighty-two.

Oscar wanted with a passion to please listeners. It had been that way from the beginning of his life at the piano. He always reached out. He wowed the kids at Montreal High with his thunderous solos for the Victory Serenaders. Decades later, a pianist with just one fully functioning hand, Oscar still sought communication with his audiences.

On June 30, 2010, Queen Elizabeth II unveiled a statue of Oscar, which stands in front of Ottawa's National Arts Centre. The statue's sculptor, Ruth Abernathy, shown chatting with the queen and Prince Philip, based the piano on Oscar's own instrument, though it's not an exact replica of the ninety-seven key Bösendorfer in the music room at the Peterson home.

The expression on Oscar's face as he performed was intent and focused. He looked like a man searching for the best way to express a piece of music. It was a serious business, and Oscar wanted the audience to understand that he was on a quest on their behalf.

He rarely laughed when he played. That sometimes changed when Ray Brown was on bass. Brown liked to find a gag or joke in the music, and he could get a rise out of Oscar. But Oscar's first concern was about intensity, a fact that his audiences latched on to. They sensed all too well that Oscar longed for communion.

Everybody who heard Oscar felt awed by his technique and power. But it was his insistence on audience communication that took him a step further, making Oscar Peterson a most rare jazz musician. He was beloved in life and still in death.

SELECTED BIBLIOGRAPHY

Balliett, Whitney. *The Sound of Surprise: 46 Pieces on Jazz*. Dutton. 1959.

Gilmore, John. *Swinging in Paradise: The Story of Jazz in Montreal*. Véhicule Press. 1988.

Lees, Gene. *Oscar Peterson: The Will to Swing*. Lester & Orpen Dennys. 1988.

Peterson, Oscar. *A Jazz Odyssey: The Life of Oscar Peterson*. Continuum. 2002.

Teachout, Terry. *Pops: A Life of Louis Armstrong*. Houghton Mifflin Harcourt. 2009.

Ulanov, Barry. *A History of Jazz in America*. Viking. 1952.

The Song Is You: Best of the Verve Songbooks. Verve. A collection of Oscar Peterson recordings from 1952 to 1959 of songs by Cole Porter, George Gershwin, and other composers from the Great American Songbook. Oscar is accompanied by Ray Brown, Herb Ellis, and Ed Thigpen.

The Oscar Peterson Trio at the Stratford Shakespearian Festival. Verve. Oscar, Ray Brown, and Herb Ellis recorded in concert at the 1956 festival in Stratford, Ontario.

Night Train. Verve. A 1962 recording of swinging, bluesy numbers by the trio of Oscar, Ray Brown, and Ed Thigpen.

Motions & Emotions. MPS. Oscar in 1968 with a string orchestra playing pop songs of the period. Arranged and conducted by Claus Ogerman.

Exclusively for My Friends. Verve. Recordings from 1963 to 1968, made in Villingen, Germany. Some tracks feature Oscar in solo; others are with varying personnel, including Ray Brown and Ed Thigpen.

If You Could See Me Now: The Oscar Peterson Quartet. Pablo. A 1983 recording of Oscar with guitarist Joe Pass, bassist Niels Pedersen, and drummer Martin Drew.

The Legendary Oscar Peterson Trio Live at the Blue Note. Telarc. A 1990 recording at the New York jazz club with Oscar, Ray Brown, and Herb Ellis together again.

A Summer Night in Munich. Telarc. 1999. Oscar with his "United Nations" quartet: Niels Pedersen (Denmark) on bass, Martin Drew (England) on drums, Ulf Wakenius (Sweden) on guitar, and Oscar (Canada) at the piano.

SOURCES

The author is grateful to the following authors for the quotations from their books, which are indicated below:

CHAPTER TWO

Quotations from Daisy Peterson

"*We kids didn't realize ...*" Page 13

"*The band was a mishmash ...*" Page 14

"*From that time on ...*" Page 18

Lees, Gene. *Oscar Peterson: The Will to Swing.* Lester & Orpen Dennys. 1988.

Quotation from Oliver Jones

"*I'm sick ...*" Page 20

Lees, Gene. *Oscar Peterson: The Will to Swing.* Lester & Orpen Dennys. 1988.

CHAPTER THREE

Quotation from Dizzy Gillespie

"*Charlie Parker ...*" Page 29

Gillespie, Dizzy. *To Be or Not to Bop.* Doubleday. 1979.

CHAPTER FOUR

Quotations from Lou Hooper

"*You know, Oscar ...*" Page 35

"*Liszt must ...*" Page 35

Peterson, Oscar. *A Jazz Odyssey: The Life of Oscar Peterson.* Continuum. 2002.

Quotations from Oscar Peterson

"*He brought into my life ...*" Page 37

"*He showed me ...*" Page 42

Peterson, Oscar. *A Jazz Odyssey: The Life of Oscar Peterson.*
Continuum. 2002.

CHAPTER FIVE

Quotation from Johnny Holmes

"*The guys called out ...*" Page 55

Gilmore, John. *Swinging in Paradise: The Story of Jazz in
Montreal.* Véhicule Press. 1988.

Quotation from Daniel Peterson

"*The only condition ...*" Page 57

Peterson, Oscar. *A Jazz Odyssey: The Life of Oscar Peterson.*
Continuum. 2002.

Quotation from Hugh Joseph

"*Well, you'll have to ...*" Page 58

Lees, Gene. *Oscar Peterson: The Will to Swing.* Lester & Orpen
Dennys. 1988.

Quotation from Lil Peterson

"*Oscar was still ...*" Page 59

Lees, Gene. *Oscar Peterson: The Will to Swing.* Lester & Orpen
Dennys. 1988.

CHAPTER SIX

Quotation from Norman Granz

"*What I thought ...*" Page 66

Balliett, Whitney. *The Sound of Surprise: 46 Pieces in Jazz.*

Dutton. 1959.

Quotation from Whitney Balliett

"... *handmaiden Peterson into fame*" Page 68

Balliett, Whitney. *The Sound of Surprise: 46 Pieces in Jazz.*
Dutton. 1959.

Quotation from Oscar Peterson

"*I was the kid...*" Page 68

Lees, Gene. *Oscar Peterson: The Will to Swing.* Lester & Orpen
Dennys. 1988.

CHAPTER SEVEN

Quotation from man in the Alberta Lounge

"*With your kind of talent ...*" Page 78

Lees, Gene. *Oscar Peterson: The Will to Swing.* Lester & Orpen
Dennys. 1988.

Quotations from Oscar Peterson

"*I knew for certain ...*" Page 83

"*I'd say your instrument ...*" Page 84

Peterson, Oscar. *A Jazz Odyssey: The Life of Oscar Peterson.*
Continuum. 2002.

CHAPTER EIGHT

Quotation from Herb Ellis

"*We reached ...*" Page 89

Lees, Gene. *Oscar Peterson: The Will to Swing.* Lester & Orpen
Dennys. 1988.

Quotation from Herb Ellis

"... *a spiritual awakening* ..." Page 95

Lees, Gene. *Waiting for Dizzy: Fourteen Jazz Portraits.* Oxford. 1991.

Quotation from Art Tatum

"*As long as I'm alive* ..." Page 101

Lees, Gene. *Oscar Peterson: The Will to Swing.* Lester & Orpen Dennys. 1988.

Quotations from Oscar Peterson

"*Only a little music* ..." Page 103

"*I was just so intent* ..." Page 104

Lees, Gene. *Oscar Peterson: The Will to Swing.* Lester & Orpen Dennys. 1988.

CHAPTER NINE

Quotations from Oscar Peterson

"*It is only now* ..." Page 111

"*Sure* ..." Page 113

Peterson, Oscar. *A Jazz Odyssey: The Life of Oscar Peterson.* Continuum. 2002.

CHAPTER TEN

Quotation from Oscar Peterson

"*On our worst night* ..." Page 120

Lees, Gene. *Waiting For Dizzy: Fourteen Jazz Portraits.* Oxford. 1991.

CHAPTER ELEVEN

Quotation from man in concert hall in Copenhagen, Denmark
"You like it?..." Page 140
Lees, Gene. *Oscar Peterson: The Will to Swing.* Lester & Orpen
Dennys. 1988.

Quotation from Oscar Peterson
"Oh my, I found ..." Page 146
Peterson, Oscar. *A Jazz Odyssey: The Life of Oscar Peterson.*
Continuum. 2002.

Quotation from Oscar Peterson
"I think My Favorite Instrument ..." Page 149
Lees, Gene. *Oscar Peterson: The Will to Swing.* Lester & Orpen
Dennys. 1988.

Quotation from Oscar Peterson
"Sandy became ..." Page 150
Peterson, Oscar. *A Jazz Odyssey: The Life of Oscar Peterson.*
Continuum. 2002.

CHAPTER TWELVE

Quotation from Oscar Peterson
"I went into a sort of morass ..." Page 159
Peterson, Oscar. *A Jazz Odyssey: The Life of Oscar Peterson.*
Continuum. 2002.

PHOTO CREDITS

Page VI: Canada-Wide

Page 8:   Canadian Pacific Railway Archives. Image #A21396.

Page 12:   City of Toronto Archives. Fonds 91268.

Page 16:   Canadian Pacific Railway Archives. Image #A21395.

Page 25:   Paul J. Hoeffler

Page 28:   Gale Research

Page 30:   Harold Robinson

Page 34:   Ken Elliott

Page 40:   Hungarian National Museum

Page 47:   CBS Records

Page 49:   Capitol Records

Page 51:   Verve Records

Page 53:   Concordia University Archives

Page 64:   Verve Records

Page 69:   Verve Records

Page 72:   Canada-Wide

Page 86:   Roy McMurtry

Page 90:   Don Newlands

Page 94:   Canada-Wide

Page 98:   Canada-Wide

Page 104:   Don Newlands

Page 109:   Howard Morehead

Page 110:   Phil Nimmons

Page 112:   Phil Nimmons

Page 118:   John Reeves

Page 121:   John Reeves

Page 128:   Pablo Records

Page 131:   Canada-Wide

Page 138:   Canada-Wide

Page 145:   Pablo Records

Page 164:   Trevor Lush

INDEX

Italics on page numbers indicate photo captions.

9/2012